2

With Man in Mind
An Interdisciplinary Prospectus
for Environmental Design

Constance Perin

J. Wheeler

The MIT Press
Cambridge, Massachusetts,
and London, England

Second printing, January 1972

First MIT Press Paperback Edition, January 1972

ISBN 0 262 16042 0 (hardcover)

ISBN 0 262 66016 4 (paperback)

Library of Congress catalog card number: 76-123251

At the present time the widest gap in knowledge is that which exists between humanistic and nonhumanistic subjects. The breach will disappear, the gap be filled, and science be manifest as an operating unity in fact and not merely in idea when the conclusions of impersonal nonhumanistic science are employed in guiding the course of distinctively human behavior, that, namely, which is influenced by emotion and desire in the framing of means and ends; for desire, having ends-in-view, and hence involving valuations, is the characteristic that marks off human from nonhuman behavior. On the other side, the science that is put to distinctively human use is that in which warranted ideas about the nonhuman world are integrated with emotion as human traits. In this integration not only is science itself *a* value (since it is the expression and the fulfilment of a special human desire and interest) but it is the supreme means of the valid determination of all valuations in all aspects of human and social life.

John Dewey, *Theory of Valuation,* 1939.

Acknowledgments

The original encouragement of Bernard P. Spring has been an invaluable impetus for my trying over these last four years to get this book written. A Fulbright fellowship in 1968–1969 enabled me to write the first draft, at the Bartlett School of Architecture, University College, London. The Ford Foundation made it possible to finish the book, thanks to the encouragement of Louis Winnick, and Jack Meltzer of the Center for Urban Studies at the University of Chicago provided the right surroundings for doing it. In between, however, was the crucial ingredient of encouragement from the readers of that ragged draft, and I am ever grateful to them for such generosity and their criticisms: Dagfinn Aas, Jarl E. Dyrud, Nathan Glazer, Harold Horowitz, Alexander H. Leighton, Kevin Lynch, Martin Rein, Maryrose and Saul Rogolsky, Walter Segal, Alvin L. Schorr, Maurice R. Stein, and Anselm L. Strauss.

Ernest Callenbach devoted extraordinary effort to putting the writing into better shape. Bette Howland shared her writer's support, advice, and graceful phrasing. Joyce Thompson of The MIT Press gave the manuscript far more than due care.

May 1970
Chicago, Illinois

Introduction

Architects and planners may be heard to ask, "Why are people so stubborn or misguided as not to use the places and spaces we design—either not at all or not in the right way?" People may be heard to ask, "Why are architects and planners so insensitive in what they put up and expect us to live with? Why do they so often leave out just what we think is so important?" The reasons for both questions lie in the way we have been going about designing the built environment; to do something about having a more compatible environment will require a revolution in theory and practice. I am suggesting here one direction for change quite specifically, so that the criticisms and emendations it invites can eventually become that revolution. The ferment is upon us, among laymen as well as among professionals. But ferment is not direction.

The direction I propose is toward uncovering a means for filling the conceptual gap between what we do to make and change the environment and what people require from their environment. Abstractly, I am suggesting a theory of human nature for environmental design. Concretely, some workable approaches are discussed that can be put to use now. As a whole, I hope to have sketched a scaffolding connecting ideas of the human sciences with the issues dealt with by environmental design. Conferences, symposia, and vast bibliographies keep exhorting toward "interdisciplinary collaboration," but the specifics of how to collaborate have been elusive. The catchphrases we share now across disciplines have not proved useful, and the need pervasively felt is for new ground on which an authentic collaboration can occur, toward action. There is no doubt, moreover, that our whole culture's transformation from the rhetorical to the scientific—in attitude even if not in fact—has also been occurring within the design professions. There is more to be gained, it is thought, from being explicit, stating intentions, searching for regularities, making measurements than from pronouncing still another aesthetic manifesto. But for the problems environmental designers handle, the quest must be for a humane rationality, not a narrowly defined "scientific" one.

I hope to interest social and behavioral scientists and the clients for new environments toward awareness of and involvement in specifying the human properties any new physical environment is to respond to. Every addition to or change in the physical environment depends on them. In architecture and urban design they are expressed in the design program which gives the numbers of people to be accommodated, the amount of space they need, and their values, priorities, and goals. But for the most part, in the way we go about designing the environment today, these statements are written and followed by the physical designers in the absence of a fully expressive set of specifications by the client or the ultimate inhabitants. Abandonment of this prerogative—one they may not have known they have—accounts for much of our displeasure with what gets built. It accounts as well for the consistently unsatisfactory means of "citizen participation" in the planning and renewal programs of our cities.

It would be fashionable to blame planners and architects for so much brand-new environmental pollution. But they have come by their power through the failure of others to be active participants. Some working designers—and most especially students of architecture, landscape architecture, and city planning —will welcome a more vital collaboration with clients, laymen, and human scientists. But because of differences in traditions and education, collaboration will come uneasily on all sides even if strong measures are taken soon in design education, in the practice of large architectural firms, in the conduct of public planning and citizen participation programs, and in the systems of incentives and career reward in the human sciences. The human sciences are asked, once again, to meet the question of how they define the problems deserving their energies and what kinds of new knowledge they think appropriate to strive for. Whether there will be a cadre of human scientists willing to work across disciplinary boundaries—and create a sustained tradition—is as yet unknown. I have tried to introduce from the human sciences only those ideas already being worked with, hoping to illustrate a genuinely common interest between them and environmental design. With the questioning of my epistemology, perhaps collaboration will finally begin.

Within the last thirty years or so the pendulum has swung from belief to disbelief that the social and behavioral sciences could be the source of wisdom for environmental designers. During this time, sociologists looking mainly into the relationship between housing conditions and social interaction found that the physical environment was not so influential as other factors. They turned their interests elsewhere. Then when the spate of urban renewal projects and new highways in the 1950s were found to have detrimental consequences for social and individual well-being, the interdisciplinary effort became more critical than collaborative, and raised the hope, still largely unfulfilled, that preventive measures could be introduced on the basis of new insights. In the 1960s poverty and political powerlessness were found to be the factors influential on unwelcome consequences of environmental changes for urban and black populations especially, and so professionals not only in the social sciences but in environmental design as well began to use their expertise as "advocates" for deprived groups in the arena of public policymaking. Another kind of active route is proposed here that may satisfy both their commitments to human well-being and to their chosen professions.

There is the argument, "We know the right things to do—we just need more money and higher priorities for them." But we do not, I believe, yet know what these right things are. A means of visualizing the future of man in his environment that brings together the inevitable inventions of science and technology with our increasing insights into human development and fulfillment is missing. Our future is marked out as one in which we will have to be building at a rate and quantity greater than ever before. We will have to master industrialized systems of building, and simply because of the array of technological advances we will be able to command, our responsibility is even greater than before to bring humanly developed knowledge into human service. But less and less does the designer know the people to live in the environment he makes. Somehow, he must.

The alternative to designing the environment with man in mind is to do it with power, greed, and self-aggrandizement in mind. Professional architects and planners are not even called upon for any advice by the majority of developers and speculators who, among others, shape so much of the built environment. Little is said in this book about these inescapable realities of power and money, but not out of naïveté or a lack of concern: to the contrary. The terrible facts of how both are used have impelled me to take time out to look for countervailing ideas and methods, as another kind of polemic entirely, one that tries to define a useful common language for our arguments, as citizens and as professionals, to keep man more clearly in mind.

1

The Limitations of Theory
in Environmental Design Today

In trying to join the mutual interests of sociology, anthropology, and psychology with those of environmental design, we seem to have reached an impasse even as we have become the most alert to collaborative possibilities. Collaboration is sparse, and even then, inadequately productive. Why is it that what seems just a simple matter of getting together—an idea born of common sense—is so complex and difficult? If the situation is to change, this has to be discussed from the points of view of both designers and human scientists. On my side of the collaboration, I find among environmental designers a mixture of eagerness, doubt, and impatience. On the other side, I notice among human scientists a mixture of eagerness, disappointment, and detachment.

What are the sources of the impasse? Does understanding them give us a new basis for working together? The sketchy background I outline as a context for these questions is not only subject to all kinds of qualifications and exceptions, it is also in flux, undergoing change and experiment wherever the impasse is constantly experienced—in design education, in action programs, and in research.

The Mutual Misapprehension of Design and Science

What is considered to be "knowledge" or "truth" and what is thought to be the means of achieving it differs considerably between the human sciences and environmental design in terms of a general outlook. Individuals involved in each may arrive at mutual understanding, but educational traditions—in architecture especially—tend to stand in the way.

The "environmental designer" is really two types of professional, qualified by two types of professional education. The first type, the urban and architectural designer, is trained in architecture or landscape architecture, and perhaps city planning. He draws up graphic, physical plans for a city, neighborhood, site, or single building. Economic and social data will determine much about these plans, but he mostly relies on others to gather and analyze them. The scale of environment he works with covers the full range, but he does not perform the same kind of work at each scale: plans for a city will show a general relation among all of the various physical elements, though limited detail may be shown for any one of them; plans for a site will show specific locations for each building and path, with much detail for all elements, such as the tree species to be planted and a cost analysis of the entire project. A building plan is highly detailed as well, down to beam widths and type of window glass. Although there are exceptions in practice, the way in which I use the term "urban and architectural designer" excludes the designer who works at a scale larger than the site (although the site can be extensive—such as the Government Center–Scollay Square area in Boston, or a 250-acre "neighborhood").

In architecture, the European *beaux-arts* tradition emphasized the "apprentice" method of learning in the atelier of a master, and today design faculty at schools of architecture are likely to carry on lively practices in which their students may also find jobs. Architectural ideas are embodied more in the personal credo of men and their experiences with buildings than in theory or research. This tradition of both craft and art perpetuates itself.

The table shows the average percentage of total credits devoted to each subject in the graduate and undergraduate programs of schools of architecture.[1] If a student has had no formal course work in any social or behavioral science or in any of the humanities (including, presumably, philosophy), then he will not get it as a graduate student. These courses at the undergraduate level are likely to be standard, introductory surveys.

The core of "architectural design" is studio work, where the student learns by doing: he is assigned problems in designing various kinds of buildings under what amounts to tutelage, head to head with the instructor over his drawings, talking with pencils. The instructors who devise the problems may also provide reading lists of works from many sources, and these recommenda-

	Undergraduate	Graduate
	(Averages of percentages)	
Architectural Design	26 percent	44 percent
Visual Studies	9	7
Social Science	3	0
Humanities	8	0
Electives	9	1

[1] *A Study of Education for Environmental Design,* sponsored by the American Institute of Architects, co-directors Robert L. Geddes and Bernard P. Spring, Princeton University, December 1967; Appendix, "The Curricula of 74 Schools of Architecture in the United States," data gathered between January 1966 and June 1967.

tions often include works in the social and behavioral sciences, clustered around those few human scientists who have written about the social and psychological implications which environments seem to have for people. Robert Gutman, a sociologist who has been studying closely "what schools of architecture expect from sociology," says that even when the architecture student takes one of several kinds of sociology courses he "himself bears the burden of extracting their implications for design and building problems; if not forced to do this work of interpretation on his own, without benefit of advice or assistance from the sociology instructor, then he does so with the help of other architecture students. . . ." But without exegesis by those trained to question and explain their own field, misinterpretation and ordinary noncomprehension result in the expectation of a sure and certain sociological knowledge of cause and effect, right and wrong, best and worst. Gutman says

Students and teachers turn to the sociologist in the hope that his subject matter will enable them to resolve ethical and evaluative issues which arise in studio work. . . . Ethical questions also arise from the differing needs of clients and users, or whenever the scheme involves a decision about the relative significance of individual and public requirement for building. . . . The moral, political and intellectual self-confidence which enabled architects in the past to prescribe specific utopian solutions to the problems of civic disorder, family life, industrial chaos, and urban blight has diminished. Like the members of most other professions and disciplines, architects are now ethical relativists, confused about what is good or bad for man, for the community, and for society. They turn to the sociologist in the hope that his discipline has somehow been spared this form of demoralization. The architect expects the sociology teacher either to be able to prescribe the values which buildings should express or to provide him with an efficient and fool-proof method through which such prescriptions can be developed.[2]

The "city and regional planner" as the other type included in the generic term "environmental designer" may have been trained in architecture as well as in city planning, but within the past several years especially, he is more likely to have had his undergraduate work in the social sciences—economics, sociology, anthropology. Unlike the "first professional degree" in architec-

[2] Robert Gutman, "What Schools of Architecture Expect From Sociology," Report No. 6, Urban Studies Center, Rutgers—The State University, April 28, 1967, p. 14 (since published in *Journal of Architectural Education*, March 1968, pp 69–83).

ture, which is a bachelor of architecture usually achieved in five years, city and regional planning is a graduate degree program only (although undergraduate curricula are increasingly offering an "urban studies" concentration). The master's degree is the first professional credential, usually a two-year program beyond the B.A. The teachers are likely to hold doctoral degrees in sociology, economics, geography, political science, and city and regional planning. Though they may also have consulting practices in which their students work, their interest in academic research keeps them more naturally connected to the university than the architecture teachers.

Certain subspecialties of engineering are developing into city planning subjects—transportation systems, waste disposal, water and air resources. Faculty teaching engineering and structural subjects to both architects and planners may also have consulting practices, but they and architectural historians, for example, are more likely to be "academics"; they are also likely to have less interest in the human sciences than teachers of design.

The city planner will also work at the smaller scale of environment, as in redesigning the "gray area" of an older city, but his claim to a particular profession lies in his concern with interrelationships of environment at all scales, from the block to the region. The city and regional planner takes into account economic and social facts of past and present in order to suggest their future. He also draws up graphic, physical plans for a city or region to show the location and interrelation of land uses, transportation networks, parks, and other community facilities. Because these plans are drawn in terms of the particular political entity trying to direct its future, they have come to include policies about welfare and education and employment; and the city planner, increasingly, is drawing up programs deploying human and fiscal resources to implement them. They may have little or nothing to do with making or changing the built environment.

These differences in the scales at which environmental designers work are at the same time qualitative differences in the kinds of decisions they make. In turn, these decisions each require their own sources of knowledge and methods of acquiring it. The decision each professional makes is which alternative he should recommend to the ultimate decisionmaker: politician or private client. The decision can be more right than wrong, and it is this quest for turning up on the right side more often than the wrong that leads the designer to learn as much as he can about likely consequences. When the environmental designer is making large-scale system decisions, such as the route for a new mass transit line through a region, he works with large-scale data systems as well; the actual reverberations of his decision are also to be felt at the very large scale. If his decision is mistaken, it may well be costly, but it is also very likely to be covered over by compensatory adaptations made by other parts of the large-scale system.

When the environmental designer is making relatively small-scale decisions, as in planning several high-rise apartment buildings on an urban site of twenty acres, he is working with a finite data system and a geographic boundary. What he decides stays decided, in concrete and brick: pathways, entrances, loading areas, greenery, playgrounds, laundry rooms, apartment size and layout, access roads. Because this designer *can* know about his finite population at a level of detail not accessible to the large-scale system designer, it might be assumed that he *does* know. The fact that he most often does not is the reason for this book. The most detailed information he is likely to work with is financial: how many dollars can be spent per square feet of building and site. It is not even "economic" data, which might discuss costs in terms of benefits, for example—but simply and strictly dollars available and income to be returned via rents or sales.

Obstacles to Communication. If we take some liberty with the complexities of the design process, we can compare an abstraction of it with an abstraction—similarly free—of the human scientist's thought processes.

To produce a plan, the designer has to make a series of decisions uniting in an unambiguous and definite statement—lines on paper translatable into three dimensions. To have arrived at a plan, the designer has to decide among an enormous range of possibilities in size, shape, location, materials, proportion, cost. He—or his team—alone will be working on that particular problem at that time. All his training is directed toward producing and defending a single set of plans—called in the design professions, in fact, a "solution." His solution is the more praiseworthy the more it is unique. The role of publications in architecture, for example, is to a great extent to maintain these sanctions, expressing disapproval for imitative or derivative work. If the architect has misunderstood science and interprets it as reason, which he thinks drives out intuition—his special preserve—he may even pride himself on offering no substantiation for his decisions beyond his own poetic or aesthetic. Although the techniques used by science might be well understood and put to use (rigorous analysis of a problem into its parts, for example), architecture makes no pretense to being a science. Materials, stresses, joints, equipment, lighting, and so on, are thought of in terms similarly occupying physics, optics, and mathematics, but this is more aptly described as technical, a matter of technique, than as scientific.[3]

City and regional planners are likely to have had more training in (and more natural sympathy for) scientific method; and substantiation is usually indispensable to their kinds of plans, including as they do projections and estimates of socioeconomic, demographic, and fiscal conditions. But they too are decision-makers; they may propose alternatives, but they must recommend the one to be followed.

The social and behavioral scientist—the human scientist—lives in a quite different milieu. Although he too is preoccupied with alternatives and likelihoods, the reason is different: his same problems—of juvenile delinquency or bureaucratic behavior—are dealt with by many others at the same time, and whatever he claims to see and conclude is open to discussion from many other points of view. The publicness of investigation and interpretation is, in fact, an invitation to other scientists to replicate his work. He constructs his "proofs" as rigorously as possible so as to circumscribe the variables under test; he claims no more from his research than is contained in its original purpose. He develops new analytic techniques under the umbrella of a theory or hypothesis. Ultimately, he is interested in predicting or forecasting the behavior of a class of phenomena as a consequence of changed conditions. The case study—the study of the unique—is simply for him a preliminary to the identification of characteristics that larger-scale research might show to be universal, and he looks askance at extrapolation.

And so, it is no surprise if a common complaint of collaborators

[3] "Generally speaking, the response of the schools has been to place increased emphasis on the academic, always at the expense of the craft component of the field. . . . Modern architectural problems can no more be solved by carpentry than could space craft be built by blacksmiths. The shift in emphasis away from craftsmanship, however, has been more toward technology than toward a truly scientific investigation of architecture." James Marston Fitch, *American Building: 1. The Historical Forces That Shaped It* (Boston: Houghton Mifflin, 1966), Second edition, p. 312.

is that they simply do not communicate. The contrasts in thinking are marked. Theory derived from quantities of data is necessarily a static abstraction of the data; designing handles the ongoing or dynamic interrelations of real phenomena. Theory explaining events must attempt a universality under given conditions; each designing effort is unique in extent, terrain, and degree. Theory in social life seeks to describe tendencies and habits as invariant rules or as dependent variables; environments are themselves new opportunities and changes from what has been. Theory in social organization classifies at a macroscale across the whole of society; designing is mainly a microscale event. Theory in the human sciences demands a value-free stance; designing is itself a value-laden commitment. Theory in the human sciences reflects the organization of the disciplines working to discover it and is consequently partial, segmented, and fractional; designing by its very nature is done with the whole environment in mind, as a system dealt with simultaneously.

Out of practical experience in trying to overcome these obstacles to communication, Gutman suggests that "the enthusiasm in many schools of architecture and among many practitioners for using sociology is unwarranted unless it is based on a serious awareness of how difficult it is intellectually at the present time to bring these two fields together."[4] Broady, a British sociologist, has also involved himself deeply in collaborative efforts with architects and planners:

The disposition which I am criticising ["architectural determinism"] has its roots deep in the intellectual bias of the architectural profession. . . . Nor does the architect's training help him to understand, except in a very superficial way, the approach of the social scientist to the kind of problems he is interested in. Sociologists, it is true, are invited to give short courses of lectures in many architectural schools. But they are usually expected to contribute on such a narrow, vocationally-oriented tack that it is difficult for them to communicate so that it sinks in what social theory is all about, how it is established and by what criteria it should be evaluated. . . . students, therefore, tend to get a general notion of how social surveys are conducted but . . . they usually fail to appreciate that a survey forms only part of a sociological argument and that it is in order to provide particular kinds of evidence for such arguments that surveys are undertaken. In my opinion, it is this imbalance between a rigorous training in visual and a superficial training in social scientific thinking that makes it possible for architectural students to accept a deterministic

4 Gutman, "What Schools of Architecture Expect From Sociology," p. 20.

answer to the complex problem of how social organisation and architectural design interact. . . ."[5]

One way to understand the environmental designer is to see him as a policymaker, similar to policymakers in Congress and the mayor's office. To the extent that he is faced with justifying his recommendations, the designer shares the sticky question of the ways in which human scientists have intended their research versus the way it is perceived. The scientist's research has been undertaken to demonstrate the range of variables likely to be involved in a problem and the relations among them, qualitative and quantitative. He views his research as having no necessary connection with impending decisions. He must also advance knowledge within his discipline, if he wants the good regard of his colleagues, and so he may even devalue the useful aspects of his work. The policymaker, being in the business of making decisions, looks to research for "the answer"—that is, the "right" decision, the one that will actually have the consequences he seeks. Millikan has concluded that if the policymaker wants advice about what to do he would get better help from the person with wide experience and demonstrated understanding than from the intellectual skills and techniques of the social scientist. What it is that the social sciences can do, says Millikan, is to make explicit the implicit concepts and assumptions of ordinary practical judgment, test their generality, and in that way be able to set forth with precision the circumstances within which they are valid. So, he says, social science research can illuminate the variety of forces at work, place limits on the range of possible outcomes, force implicit and partial judgments into explicit form so they can be systematically examined, and explore the internal consistency of a variety of intuitive expectations. "Thus, although social science cannot often predict, it may make very important contributions to effective prediction. Social science cannot replace intuition and experience, but it can greatly enrich them, clarify them, and make them more general."[6]

A policy is a "best guess" about the consequences of taking action, and all share equally—or ought to—in the risks of being "wrong." But in environmental design demands are often made

5 Maurice Broady, *Planning for People* (London: Bedford Square Press of The National Council of Social Service, 1968), p. 16.

6 Max F. Millikan, "Inquiry and Policy: The Relation of Knowledge to Action," in *The Human Meaning of the Social Sciences*, edited by Daniel Lerner (Cleveland and New York: Meridian Books, 1959), p. 166.

for accurate forecasts as a condition of using research findings at all, and when the social scientist sets limitations on the validity of his findings, the designer does not applaud this scientific veracity, but instead becomes disappointed and distrustful. He may also complain that social science research seems to be little more than common sense systematized, and although he may not be so far wrong, he fails to understand science as an enterprise whose very purpose is to try to prove and disprove our common sense about our world.

And so because deciding is a main responsibility for the designer and the least responsibility for the human scientist as researcher, we find designers filling the breach with simple assertions about the consequences of what they do, based on, as it were, the furniture of their minds and the inspirations of their intuitions. We are enriched by some of their extraordinary intuitions and assertions. But many have been so banal and so disconnected from the real world as to have provided the banal and unreal environments we rail against. The human scientist contributes to banality when he retreats into a self-imposed version of "truth" in his field and fails to, as Gutman puts it, "assume the kind of risk that the architect takes every day when he makes a design decision based on incomplete and fragmentary knowledge."[7]

Truman explains some self-containment in the social sciences as essential to their progress:

Some increased isolation of the social sciences from each other and some increased obstacles to a direct pertinence of the social sciences to public policy are clearly unavoidable. A growth in rigor leads inevitably to a greater self-consciousness in a discipline, to the setting of priorities and agendas of research in terms of the assumptions and requirements of the discipline (as seen by the practitioners themselves), and consequently to remoteness from each other and from the full, complex reality of problems in the political arena. The contrast, of course, is not between a simpler, less pretentious set of social sciences fully sensitive and pertinent to the range of policy, on the one hand, and a more sophisticated group of disciplines paradoxically rendered socially impotent by an increase in power that is purely scholastic, on the other. It is rather between a set of presciences scarcely distinguishable from the folklore and wisdom operating in the market place and a group of sciences or nascent sciences that have attempted to set themselves intellectually manageable prob-

7 Gutman, "What Schools of Architecture Expect From Sociology," p. 24.

lems by abstracting in various degrees from reality through discarding some of its features, and hence they have created the problem of relevance as they have separated themselves from folklore, from each other, and from the totality of the policy complex.[8]

Accepting that as the trend we are in, this book as a whole proposes one way out of the impasse. Instead of relying on exhortation to change people, I have redefined the problems in the hope that people will become newly interested in them, through clarification of environmental design issues in the light of those same "agendas of research" human scientists have set for themselves.

Theory and Findings at the Drawing Board

Insofar as it tries to understand and control its human consequences, environmental design relies on the same questions which occupy sociology, political science, anthropology, and psychology, assuming for the most part they will fit its purposes. These disciplines, strictly speaking, have meant their propositions and generalizations to be satisfactory to their own history and development, and they make common cause with other fields only when pushed. Those constructs unique to environmental design cluster mainly around the formal and aesthetic properties of space, volume, location, and style. These physical characteristics have been assumed to carry meanings for human behavior in the same terms used by the social and behavioral sciences as we know them. Research has shown they may and they may not. What is missing is a theory of human nature unique to environmental design.

The tendency has been to accept the formulations of sociologists and anthropologists as they view the family, occupational roles, and various socioeconomic characteristics, as a guide to matching up people's identities and the artifacts to surround their relationships. And so, the concern in design has been housing, not how families live; and transportation, not why people move around every day. Schorr comments:

A final reason that the impact of physical housing may tend currently to be understated has to do with the stage of sophistication of research into housing. The research that is available . . . is partial and requires to be pieced together. A conception has yet to be developed that sees man in relation to his physical

8 David B. Truman, "The Social Sciences and Public Policy," *Science*, Vol. 160, 3 May 1968, pp. 508–512.

environment. Until such a scheme is developed, and research adapted to it, we shall not fully perceive the relationship of man to shelter. Meanwhile, we shall build houses.[9]

The vocabulary the designer ordinarily uses to explain the human consequences of what he has created applies the adjective "human" to modify use, need, function, aspiration, and, of course, scale—rarely with further specification. The jargon of the critics simply juxtaposes the adjective "inhuman" to describe buildings and situations made by man that are felt in some way to be destructive to dignity or the social order. The critics too fail to supply further details: *how* are they destructive, in what particular ways, relative to what ideas about being human? The maxim of Vitruvius in the first century A.D. for architectural "firmness, commodity, and delight" is a poetic context for what we build and live with today. But until we have the ability to specify contemporary meanings, we will have no bill of particulars with which to change our habits of design. No site plan or building design is explained in its intentions toward people by reference to the ideas of theorists such as Sigmund Freud, Ruth Benedict, George Mead, Erik Erikson, B. F. Skinner, Jerome Bruner. The point seems an exaggeration, but ought we be so certain that it will always seem that way? What, then, in current social and behavioral science theory is furnishing the environmental designer's mind with criteria for explanations and evaluations? What seem to be the advantages and limitations of this theory for the purpose of conceiving a new environment? How does the way in which research findings are made and stated help or hinder the designer? The answers I offer are hardly complete. But they should move us toward the basis for an epistemology unique to environmental design: what do we need to know in order to design with man in mind?

Theory at the Larger Scale of Environment. In urban and regional planning, to take the larger scale of environmental design first, several theoretical bases from economics and political science especially are used in explaining the factors entering into the growth and spread of cities—explanations of such factors as the relative locations of economic activities in space, the decision-making behavior of households and firms, the transportation and communication systems as both respondents to and shapers

9 Alvin L. Schorr, *Slums and Social Insecurity*, Research Report No. 1, Division of Research and Statistics, Social Security Administration (Washington: U.S. Government Printing Office, 1963), pp. 32-33.

of growth. Explanations of the relationships between land values and rents, transportation accessibility and costs, population composition and housing supply, and regional input and output are examples of developing theory being translated into mathematical models used by planners to justify their recommendations for the numbers and placement of particular public facilities, such as mass transit, highways, new communities, and greenbelts, at the regional scale. In city planning, they are also used in justifying recommendations for land-use patterns as embodied, for example, in zoning legislation and urban renewal project authorizations. In urban design, which traces out the actual physical patterns of physical facilities on the landscape, some taxonomic concepts have been developed for the possible forms future development can take—concentrated or dispersed, linear or concentric. The scale of these theoretical and conceptual approaches is macro: urban and regional growth dynamics are being understood as an interdependent system of land, transportation, population, and industrial base.

Curiously, sociological theory has had little influence on macro-scale theory development in urban and regional planning, which has taken most of its cues from economics. The situation is not altogether satisfactory; recent work in developing a theory of urban travel behavior has concluded that "deterministic economic models, with their built-in assumptions of economic rationality, have been noteworthy for their lack of success in accounting for spatial behavior, except at a highly aggregate level. . . . Attempts to utilize variables which have been shown to be statistically related to urban travel at the aggregate level have been almost universally unsuccessful at the household level . . . factors which are important conditioners of mass group behavior (such as employment rate, median income, etc.) are devoid of behavioral meaning at a less aggregated level."[10]

Two sociologists find deficiencies in current human ecology for helping to explain man's organized relations with his environment. Kunkel finds that the nature and operation of the link between the two has so far not been clearly stated: "social organization, inadequately or grossly conceptualized, makes it difficult to indicate exactly what aspects of social life and what type of social phenomena are related to the environment." One

10 Frank E. Horton and David R. Reynolds, "Action Space Formation: A Behavioral Approach to Predicting Urban Travel Behavior," Institute of Urban and Regional Research, University of Iowa, August 1969, p. 4.

reason lies, he believes, with the scarcity of data, which makes "such an inquiry difficult and leads to the analysis of gross phenomena without adequate recognition of [their] variability and complexity."[11] Michelson finds that even orthodox theorists of human ecology produce studies that concentrate on economic variables as "the main explanatory forces," the more disappointing because they have originally claimed population, organization, environment, and technology to be the four interdependent variables in the ecological complex. In commenting on the use of Social Area Analysis, Michelson finds that because only the variable "housing condition" is made use of to represent the physical environment, this approach "says just about nothing about the physical nature of areas and its relationship to social phenomena. The word 'Area' in Social Area Analysis conveys connotations that are not fulfilled."[12] Kunkel and Michelson agree that by dealing solely with aggregated data on population the human ecologists have provided little help in explaining either the individual or the varied physical environment at the microscale. As Michelson puts it,

The human ecologists left to other disciplines whatever understanding of social structure and consequent behavior might stem from its relations with the physical environment. . . . I claim that in the interests of establishing a neat discipline, the ecologists have eliminated subjects of study which are sorely missed at present.[13]

For environmental design particularly, urban ecology has become mainly an outlook encouraging a greater number of intercorrelations of census data, losing Park's original intention to understand the city as a "product of nature, and particularly human nature."[14] The fact that a unit of analysis is still in dis-

11 John H. Kunkel, "Some Behavioral Aspects of the Ecological Approach to Social Organization," *American Journal of Sociology*, Vol. 73, No. 1, July, 1967, p. 13.
12 William Michelson, "A Parsonian Scheme for the Study of Man and Environment, or What Human Ecology Left Behind in the Dust," *Sociological Inquiry*, Vol. 38, No. 1, Spring 1968, p. 201.
13 Ibid, p. 204. Moreover, the refinement of analytic techniques and the advent of hardware makes one wish all the more that the original data categories handled more about people than the usual census sources; see Carl-Gunnar Janson, "Some Problems of Ecological Factor Analysis," in Mattei Dogan and Stein Rokkan, editors, *Quantitative Ecological Analysis in the Social Sciences* (Cambridge: M.I.T. Press, 1969), pp. 301–341.
14 Robert E. Park and Ernest W. Burgess, *The City* (Chicago: University of Chicago Press, 1925), p. 1.

pute—whether it is properly the individual or the population aggregated—would seem to mean that little conceptual progress has been made. Even the tools are underdeveloped: the boundaries of enumeration districts (the smallest areal unit in the Census next to the city block) change every ten years as the population changes, instead of staying the same and permitting automatically the most elementary ecological analysis! (Only enumeration district statistics are available for places of less than a certain size, and in metropolitan areas, such places are often the inner suburbs.)

Chapin has summed up the situation for urban and regional planning:

[The] socially rooted determinants of urban land use are less understood and frequently confused with economic determinants . . . there is a strong disposition in much of the writing on the subject to equate social influences with the economic, and social motivations of people and groups with economic motivations.[15]

Lisa Redfield Peattie, an anthropologist working in urban and regional planning, has put it even more forcefully in a review of a collection of writings on urban issues:

Taking the papers in these volumes as a sample, one might conclude that the major contribution of sociology to thinking about urban policy has been the depiction of the miseries of poverty and the discovery of "urban villagers" in the path of the bulldozers. This would no doubt be unfair. . . . But the conclusion may not be so far wrong. It might be worthwhile for sociologists to look at a collection of materials like this one . . . to treat it as a collection of data to be processed by the conceptual apparatus of sociology. How adequate is that conceptual apparatus for dealing with megalopolis descriptively and for illuminating the policy problems which arise in that institutional setting? Are not sociologists, in fact, missing some of the action?[16]

The practice of city planning itself has so concentrated on land use, on physical facilities, on municipal finance, and on rational decision-making that almost no use has been made of it as a natural source of the anthropological and sociological community studies that should complement demographic and economic analysis. Gans's *The Levittowners* and Berger's *Work-*

---

15 F. Stuart Chapin, Jr., *Urban Land Use Planning* (Urbana: University of Illinois Press, 1965), Second edition, p. 21.
16 Lisa Redfield Peattie, book review of *Taming Megalopolis: How to Manage an Urbanized World*, edited by H. Wentworth Eldredge, in *American Journal of Sociology*, Vol. 73, No. 5, March 1968, pp. 639–640.

ing-Class Suburb could stand as models for the kind of qualitative studies now missing from much city and regional planning.[17] Instead, interdisciplinary involvement in city planning has shown itself mainly as *critical,* where social scientists demonstrate what went wrong as a consequence of having changed the physical environment—as in Gans's *The Urban Villagers* and Fried's studies of the same West Enders of Boston after they moved.[18] The "model cities" approach in the federal government—of integrating the planning of physical and social action agencies or institutions of a subcommunity—is also a response to the critical literature. The universities teaching environmental design are responding with new courses concentrating on the social consequences of planning for physical change, and students are learning that a more inclusive human data base can change the nature of municipal policy in planning and renewal. The critical literature has been one source of these new pressures on environmental design to explain ahead of time just what consequences are likely, unintended as well as intended, when public power and money are being used to "promote the public interest." But the critical literature is better able to tell the politician what to avoid than to enlighten the designer about what to do.

"Economic determinism" is, then, the more usual directive for the larger-scale environmental designer. As a predictive enterprise, economics has explicitly related itself to one postulate about human nature—"self-interest." It is an attribute made to account for many consequences, and strategies are formulated on that basis in urban and regional planning as well, as they locate residences, industries, shopping centers. For one, highway networks are based on the assumption that the single end of reducing the time-costs of traveling is equally important to all people. But in the face of the evidence that people have chosen considerable dispersal, what seems to be implied instead is that lowering their time-costs may not mean as much as gaining other things (fresh air, a homogeneous social group, a setting for their

[17] Herbert J. Gans, *The Levittowners: Ways of Life and Politics in a New Suburban Community* (New York: Pantheon, 1967); Bennett Berger, *Working-Class Suburb: A Study of Auto Workers in Suburbia* (Berkeley: University of California Press, 1960).

[18] Herbert J. Gans, *The Urban Villagers* (New York: Free Press of Glencoe, 1962); Marc Fried, "Grieving for a Lost Home," in Leonard J. Duhl, editor, *The Urban Condition* (New York: Basic Books, 1963), pp. 151–171, and "Functions of the Working-Class Community in Modern Urban Society: Implications for Forced Relocation," *Journal of the American Institute of Planners,* Vol. 33, No. 2, March 1967, pp. 90–103.

possessions). Fewer highways, not more, would probably be justifiable on the basis of a more subtle and realistic analysis of the social function of location decisions. The very fact that Firey centered on cultural systems, as the link between people's motives and decisions to live where they do in the city, enabled him to explain "land use in Central Boston" so satisfactorily. He undertook his research because he found that the economists' commitment to their theory of maximum efficiency as the goal of all orderings in space of human activities "forces them to state deviations from the theory as stemming from imperfect people who make decisions out of ignorance and error."[19]

Perhaps it is simply because economic theory has organized so many complex, unobservable human decision processes into the one rubric of "self-interest" that it has achieved such standing among the social sciences. But a tidy package similar to the one in which utilitarian "economic man" is wrapped is unlikely to be available from the kinds of thinking urban and regional planning needs most for its future: Those human events and social processes which are claimed to be the basis of city and regional planning are explained inadequately. It is environmental variety that will satisfy the range of human diversity in our society; definitions of that diversity and the location of environmental elements are the special questions that urban and regional planning can help to answer. One goal for collaboration between the environmental designers working at the larger scale and social scientists, for example, might be to reduce the overwhelming variety of human behavior into a few hundred constructs of household types—to replace the simple column headings now relied on mainly because they are available.[20] Household types could be defined by differences in travel habits, the trade-

19 Walter Firey, *Land Use in Central Boston* (Cambridge: Harvard University Press, 1947), p. 21. For a largely negative view of Firey, written in 1950, see Lloyd Rodwin, "The Theory of Residential Growth and Structure," in William L. C. Wheaton, Grace Milgram, and Margy Ellin Meyerson, editors, *Urban Housing* (New York: Free Press, 1966), especially p. 77.

20 "In the area of mental illness, where the major phenomena are all abstract to begin with, what could be more reasonable than to look for the proximal causative factors in the abstract (psychosocial) environment? . . . Part of the responsibility for the disappointing results, thus far, and for the tendency to turn more to the ecological end of the causative spectrum, must be assigned to the limited character of the environmental variables so often studied. There appears to be an absence of imagination in this area and the general approach is to use demographic data and other similar data because they are available." Edward S. Rogers, "Public Health Asks of Sociology . . . ," *Science,* Vol. 159, 2 February 1968, p. 507.

offs made between time and money, shopping behavior, stage in the life cycle, the age spread of children, and so on.[21] Such data might enable macroscale planners to say with greater certainty that "some people are . . ." instead of saying "everybody is . . ." when it leads to strategies contrary to the goals of large groups.

Theory at the Smaller Scale of Environment. For the remainder of this book, the types of plans I am discussing come after those larger-scale planning decisions that allocate land uses here or there, suggest the modes of transport in the region, propose the preservation of particular natural resources. The scale is instead relatively micro: such as the dwelling unit design and site plan for five acres of two hundred low-income dwelling units; or the plans for a shopping center to serve eight thousand suburban families; or the network of transit stations being designed for a new system. There is no fixed sequence for making plans: microscale plans may be just as likely to precede those on a larger scale and perhaps even influence their content considerably. Although both types of designers work at this scale, the urban and architectural designers predominate.

It is mainly at this smaller scale that sociological theory is sought, as it has dealt with social interaction, socioeconomic differences, and social organization. I refer to this scale when I speak of the designer at his drawing board, making the decisions about apartment layout, paths, laundry rooms, play spaces, parking lots, office buildings, corridors, lavatories, and all those elements of prime importance to the people who will be living and working in the new environment. Sociology more than any other social science has concerned itself with the two streams influencing the little research there has been at this scale: the first is the early sociologists' conception of "the city" and the second is the housing reform movement that blossomed in the 1930s.

At the time of conceiving plans for a building or neighborhood the designer is very much taken up with questions about the consequences of high and low density and the concentration or spread of facilities such as schools, libraries, shops, and health facilities. Out of the original formulations of Durkheim, Wirth,

---

[21] Some new data series along this line are suggested by Raymond A. Bauer, "Social Indicators," in Stanford Anderson, editor, *Planning for Diversity and Choice,* (Cambridge: M.I.T. Press, 1968), pp. 248–249.

and Park who saw the city as an independent variable affecting the character of social life and organization, the designer has been drawing stereotyped conclusions about the life styles people have as a consequence of density, locational arrangements, and architectural style. These sociologists say that urban social life takes its character from the intensity of the relationships among the size, density, and heterogeneity of the population, and "country" was an implicit aspect of their definition of "city." The more intense each variable, the greater the social interaction of the population, but when "too great" depersonalization and superficiality result. Gans and Keller[22] have argued that contemporary urban structure makes this approach outmoded; but in the absence of any other theoretical connections being suggested between the size, density, and heterogeneity of population and the consequences of the interrelationship, designers are hard pressed to state other "social meanings" of their work, which takes so many of its cues from the size and density of populations. In these days when people can live in the country and partake of social life in the heart of the city within thirty minutes, the consequences are more obscure. High-density row housing is being built in the open country while expensive, luxury buildings are placed next to low-income housing in the city—requiring new definitions of country and of "social" interaction. Even "invasion" and "succession" as pivotal concepts of urban ecology have changed in fact, where black ghettos are populated not only by the traditional low-income in-migrants, but by the well-to-do who, for cultural and political reasons, prefer to stay put even when they have the choice. The social networks we may try to explain depend less on static characteristics of people and more on their various means of physical mobility in getting to work, shopping, attending school, visiting, and on their various degrees of economic mobility, depending on age, education, race, and income. And so, when the designer thinks about creating a "neighborhood" where social organization and interaction might flourish, he may need, but not yet find, fresh concepts and data about the quality and meaning to people of neighborhood inter-

22 Herbert J. Gans, *People and Plans: Essays on Urban Problems and Solutions* (New York: Basic Books, 1968); Suzanne Keller, *The Urban Neighborhood: A Sociological Perspective* (New York: Random House, 1968). See also Janet Abu-Lughod, "The City is Dead—Long Live the City: Some Thoughts on Urbanity (A Summary)," *The American Behavioral Scientist*, Vol. 10, No. 1, September 1966, pp. 3–5.

actions compared with those maintained despite geographical distance.[23]

Findings At the Drawing Board. The hypothesis that an intimate correlation exists between housing conditions and social and personal health has been tested by sociological research for the last several decades. The underlying hope was that better housing could decrease various ills, but the situation turns out to be more complex. Recent research has found that even the concomitance of bad housing and social pathology is not necessarily causal; in fact, the possibility is allowed that "social relationships and social solidarity are more likely to affect the way housing of any quality is used than the reverse. . . . Cohesive families living in the slums of underdeveloped areas are observed not to be adversely affected by poor housing, and they may not even see themselves as living in slums. At the same time, the benefits of housing amenities can be nullified by the fragmented and incohesive family relationships which inhibit their adequate use."[24] The standards for health that medicine can document are not in dispute—only that the medical model of "disease and cure" seems to have run its course as a productive outlook for the design of positive environments. The one significant longitudinal study of slum dwellers who moved to quality (public) housing confirmed the truth of our common sense assumptions about better versus worse housing conditions: improved housing can mean a general improvement in some important areas of life, though not all.[25] But that research has addressed the prior policy question of how much social benefit the social investment in housing will produce, which is not the issue in this discussion. Rather, the question is: when the designer is putting together an environment, what informs him about the human consequences of the decisions he

[23] One sociologist has recently rediscovered Wirth's interest in the quality of urban and rural interactions, not their quantity—but the measures used in empirical work do not tap the qualitative dimensions, and so the findings over the years have supposedly contradicted Wirth's view that there is a negative correlation between the intimacy of friendship ties and the size of the place lived in. Stanley S. Guterman, "In Defense of Wirth's 'Urbanism as a Way of Life'," *American Journal of Sociology*, Vol. 74, No. 5, March 1969, pp. 492–499.

[24] Martin Rein, "Social Science and the Elimination of Poverty," *Journal of the American Institute of Planners*, Vol. 33, No. 3, May 1967, p. 150. See also Kurt W. Back, *Slums, Projects, and People* (Durham: Duke University Press, 1962).

[25] Daniel M. Wilner, Rosabelle Price Walkley, Thomas C. Pinkerton, Matthew Tayback, *The Housing Environment and Family Life* (Baltimore: Johns Hopkins Press, 1962).

makes as a matter of course in that process? Creating and re-creating the physical environment may not be the most important thing a society does for enriching the potentialities of its members, but as long as it is being done, an integrity appropriate to it should be sought.

Designers, handling so many variables, faced with having to emphasize some and not others, are continually hoping to find an isolatable and accessible key factor. But research that identifies some dependent and independent variables does not tell the designer what he needs to know about the *whole situation*—his unique concern. That is, his decisions are likely to be tradeoffs: he maximizes one kind of space and minimizes another, or uses a less expensive material in order to allow for the highest quality lighting fixtures, or provides more facilities for preschool children than for the elderly. The virtue of one kind of tradeoff over another is most often substantiated by invoking precedent: use of a similar tradeoff in a similar situation. The use of games, where hypothetical political and economic decisionmaking is acted out, is a likely source of this kind of understanding, but as yet without a literature in environment design.[26] In his search for substantiation of this kind, the designer is more likely than not to turn to himself—his personal and professional experiences.

Unfortunately, the research that is available in this vein serves mainly to heighten the need for a new syntax of findings that the designer can understand and use. One problematic aspect is the substance of the findings themselves, when "negative correlations" appear between environment and behavior. Gutman's review of the studies designed to uncover the relationships between "site planning and social behavior" finds that they "do not make a very compelling case for the argument that the site plan is an important influence on individual behavior and collective social action."[27] The one study still cited most frequently was made by Festinger, Schachter, and Back, and in the twenty years since publication, it has never been replicated![28] What

26 A review of such simulation techniques as there are—none yet below the scale of the city—is in Peter House and Philip D. Patterson, Jr., "An Environmental Gaming-Simulation Laboratory," *Journal of the American Institute of Planners*, Vol. 35, No. 6, November 1969, pp. 383–388.

27 Robert Gutman, "Site Planning and Social Behavior," *Journal of Social Issues*, Vol. 22, No. 4, October 1966, p. 112.

28 Leon Festinger, Stanley Schachter, and Kurt Back, *Social Pressures in Informal Groups: A Study of Human Factors in Housing* (New York: Harper & Bros., 1950).

this reveals may be the generalized attitude among social scientists who, having found that the physical environment shows up as a relatively unimportant variable in social organization, turned their attentions to other hypotheses. The designers' reactions to negative correlations, on the other hand, have included pointing to the defects of the people who make the "wrong use" of their environments!

But despite negative correlations,[29] the issue for the designer remains clear: he is still having to decide about curving the streets or not, locating common meeting rooms, concentrating or dispersing large or small shopping areas, fixing the sizes of play spaces, allocating private open space—and he wants to know how to weight them. The "user studies" literature should be a major source of substantiation because it attempts to evaluate the actual human consequences of a designed environment once lived or worked in. We should be able to refer to a wide range of research evaluating housing for diverse populations in all its aspects—space, numbers of rooms, high-rise, single-family—but there is very little cumulative explanation, not only for housing but for all other types of buildings as well. Svend Riemer's studies of livability done in the 1940s could well be replicated.[30] Louis Winnick's 1957 monograph drawing out the implications for livability of housing statistics on the person-per-room ratio by comparing the 1940 and 1950 census data could be done again with profit.[31] Elisabeth Coit's evaluation of high-rise public housing, published in 1965, does not show any similar studies in her bibliography (although the FHA published "Liveability Problems of 1,000 Families" in 1945).[32] Robert Katz's two studies

[29] A most even-handed discussion of such studies is by Schorr, *Slums and Social Insecurity*. An overview of forty British and American studies is found in chapter one, Wilner et al., *The Housing Environment and Family Life*. A recent review and evaluation of many relevant past studies is in William H. Michelson, *Man and His Urban Environment: A Sociological Approach* (Reading, Mass.: Addison-Wesley Publishing Co., 1970).

[30] Svend Riemer, "Architecture for Family Living," *Journal of Social Issues*, Vol. VII, Nos. 1 and 2, 1951, pp. 140–151; and *The Modern City: An Introduction to Urban Sociology* (New York: Prentice-Hall, 1952), Chapter 16, "Housing."

[31] Louis Winnick, *American Housing and Its Use: The Demand for Shelter Space* (New York: John Wiley & Sons, 1957).

[32] Elisabeth Coit, "Report on Family Living in High Apartment Buildings," Public Housing Administration, Housing and Home Finance Agency, May 1965. See also an Australian study, Anne Stevenson, Elaine Martin, and Judith O'Neill, *High Living: A Study of Family Life in Flats* (Carlton, Victoria: Melbourne University Press, 1967).

of multifamily housing and site design[33] are each unique, as is Sim van der Ryn's of dormitory livability.[34] Clare Cooper's research, done in the last few years, into the inhabitants' attitudes toward their low density, public housing seems to be the only one of its kind.[35]

The liveliness of Great Britain in this research area is in such contrast that it must be remarked. Even discounting the national characteristic of biting wit in debate and comment, it is certain that in Great Britain the quantity and quality of serious and constructive criticism, often based on research, in architecture and city planning is superior to ours. One explanation may lie with the habits instilled by the 1947 Town and Country Planning Act which required the government to conduct "social surveys" before planning New Towns. A cadre of sociologists (Lock, Glass, et al.) developed these tools, almost immediately used to uncover attitudes toward housing types, since the government would be providing so much of it.[36] In 1961 much previous research was codified in the Ministry of Housing and Local Government's publication of *Homes for Today and Tomorrow* (the Parker Morris report), now the regulations under which public, and much private, housing is built.[37] The report gives guiding principles, recommended minimum standards, and cost implications, but all within a context of much flexibility for the architect. Immediately after the report was finished, thirty-nine houses were designed and built to gain practical experiences with the recommendations, and their advantages and problems for the inhabitants were evaluated.[38] In addition, the Building Research

[33] Robert D. Katz, *Design of the Housing Site* (Small Homes Council and Building Research Council, University of Illinois, 1966); and *Intensity of Development and Livability of Multi-Family Housing Projects: Design Qualities of European and American Housing Projects* (Washington, D.C.: Federal Housing Administration, 1963).

[34] Sim Van der Ryn, *Dorms at Berkeley: An Environmental Analysis* (University of California Center for Planning and Development, 1968); and, with Murray Silverstein, "Berkeley: How Do Students Really Live?", *Architectural Forum*, July/August 1967, pp. 91–97.

[35] Clare C. Cooper, "Some Social Implications of House and Site Plan Design at Easter Hill Village: A Case Study," Institute of Urban and Regional Development, Center for Planning and Development Research, University of California, Berkeley, 1965, mimeo.

[36] Henry Cohen, "Social Surveys as Planning Instruments for Housing: Britain," *Journal of Social Issues*, Vol. VII, Nos. 1 and 2, 1951, pp. 35–36.

[37] Ministry of Housing and Local Government, *Homes for Today & Tomorrow* (London: Her Majesty's Stationery Office, 1961), 92 pp.

[38] Ministry of Housing and Local Government, *Family Houses at West Ham: An Account of the Project with an Appraisal,* Design Bulletin 15, (London: HMSO, 1969). See also, "Housing at Ravenscroft Road, West Ham," *The Architects' Journal*, 28 October 1964, pp. 1001–1012.

Station, under the Ministry of Research and Technology, has become the center of research into inhabitants' responses to new buildings, continuously carried out by a permanent staff sociologist, architects, engineers, and planners.[39] In the Ministry of Housing, a Research and Development group with similar staff composition and research interests has recently published "The House in its Setting" which will eventually become a Ministry bulletin for the site planning of public housing.[40] *The Architects' Journal,* a weekly magazine of a commercial press, carries its own appraisals of various kinds of buildings, using both plans and site visits, raising all kinds of detailed questions about their prospects under the "ordeal of use."[41] The architects and their colleagues on the project are named: the articles are unsigned. American architectural periodicals express disapproval more by what they keep out of their pages of pictures—a tacit maneuver understood by insiders but not particularly instructive.

The prospect of having direct influence on practice is usually far more promising in Great Britain than here—one reason for the disparity in evaluative research activity between the two countries. The research is usually undertaken to provide the basis for government action in a small country whose centralized government regulations often have precedence over local regula-

39 W. V. Hole and J. J. Attenburrow, *Houses and People: A Review of User Studies at the Building Research Station* (London: HMSO, 1966); Vere Hole, *Children's Play on Housing Estates* (London: HMSO, 1966); W. V. Hole, "User Needs and the Design of Houses: The Current and Potential Contribution of Sociological Studies," Building Research Station, Current Paper 51/68, June 1968 (Garston, Watford, Hertfordshire); Phyllis Allen, "Hostel User Study," Building Research Station, Current Paper 50/68, June 1968; A. Miller and J. A. Cook, "Pedestrians and Vehicles on Housing Estates: A User Study," Building Research Station, Current Paper 23/68, March 1968.

40 Research and Development Group, Ministry of Housing, "Housing: The Home in Its Setting (Progress Report)," in *The Architects' Journal,* 11 September 1968, pp. 493–554; Sociological Research Section, Ministry of Housing and Local Government, "Housing at Coventry," *Official Architecture and Planning,* Vol. 30, No. 12, December 1967, 20 pages; Sociological Research Section, Research and Development Group, Ministry of Housing and Local Government, "Housing Single People," Final Draft, November 1966 (mimeo) 51 pages.

41 "The assessors' [of a design competition] . . . make ample use of such phrases as 'simple and satisfying,' 'better than most,' 'visual integrity,' 'feeling of crispness.' . . . The sliding scale of meaning with which such terms can be used is illustrated by what the 1967 assessors termed the 'immediate humanity' of a high rise, high density development of 346 flats and seventy-six maisonettes. . . . The relationship of the Good Design in Housing Awards to good design in housing can be demonstrated only by the ordeal of use. We are presented with a *concours d'élégance* when we need a *vingt-quatre heures du Mans," The Architects' Journal,* 11 September 1968, pp. 485–486.

tions, whose New Towns provide very nearly experimental conditions, and whose climate is much the same throughout. Another factor in this difference may be in the types of sociology practiced in each country: Great Britain still maintains an empirical outlook unencumbered by much theorizing, while in the United States the continuing search for grand theory often leads to disdain for data.

But however active this user research effort may be, it fails in its design and the syntax of its findings to answer the real need. Studies will show flat percentages of those who do and do not prefer one design feature at a time. When these preference data are also not correlated with obvious determinants, such as previous residential experience, whether the wife is working, or the age-spread of children in the household, they are very nearly useless to the designer. The research that would be most useful would put the findings in a syntax of tradeoffs: what things are likely to be given up in order to achieve others? The designer working closely with a client who can speak with one voice uses this method as a matter of course; a research literature would have to report similarly on those ultimate inhabitants designers never meet.

User research [in Great Britain] is often pilloried for its banality and focus on current needs. If it were linked to a more generalised knowledge of human behaviour and of the processes of social change, more effective predictions concerning user needs in the future might be developed. . . . The main problem is that of achieving effective communication between architects and sociologists. Too often the questions posed by architects cannot be answered directly; they have to be re-phrased and often need a good deal of fundamental research before an understanding of the real problem is achieved. . . . It is clear . . . that part of the difficulty lies in the unsatisfactory conceptual models of society which architects use, particularly concerning society, the individual and the physical environment.[42]

Gutman points out similarly sad facts of life for both sociologists and architects in the United States:

As a consequence of their own frustrating experiences, faculty members have become convinced that the architect with a conventional training simply does not know enough about the needs of clients and consumers. They expect that the information which the sociologist has acquired about user requirements will compensate for the deficiencies in traditional architectural education. . . . Given the intellectual stance of contemporary sociology, the legitimacy of the architects' demand that sociologists con-

42 Hole, "User Needs and the Design of Houses," pp. 2 and 6.

tribute useful guesses about the social consequences of design proposals must be acknowledged. Sociology's capacity to match these expectations, however, is still limited for the simple reason that until quite recently the discipline has not conducted much research on user requirements. Although the lack of a research tradition in this area constitutes an obvious explanation for the absence of meaningful information, this point is often ignored by the student and teacher of architecture. The architect tends to assume that the questions he asks can be answered on the basis of general sociological theory and research.[43]

Instead of the generalizations, exhortative principles, and inter-correlations of data in which social science findings may be couched—and which the designer may sometimes believe and believe in—what we need are findings of a kind he can integrate into specific plans for particular buildings, new communities, neighborhoods. Twenty years ago Catherine Bauer Wurster listed the *"real problems,"* as she put it, the planner and architect face in the form of an agenda for social research, as viable today as ever.[44] Twenty years ago Mumford offered homely prescriptions for research in environmental design as a "person-centered" enterprise—still well worth following.[45] But the pursuit of proof by the social sciences of facts having an existence independent of man as a psychological being (that is, toward uncovering the "structures and functions" of society) has led the environmental design disciplines to believe that this constitutes the only valid way to conceive of and have theories about man in society. Our depersonalized buildings and neighborhoods are witness to conceptions of man merely as he accumulates in aggregated roles, social structure, bureaucracy, and institutions. Even among his colleagues in sociology Homans must plead to "bring men back in," trying to convince them that sociology, anthropology, economics, and psychology are unified by their fundamental interest in the person and what he does.[46]

The end product is environmental design that takes its role as seriously as the bus driver who maintained his time schedule

43 Gutman, "What Schools of Architecture Expect From Sociology," pp. 18–19.
44 Catherine Bauer, "Social Questions in Housing and Community Planning," *Journal of Social Issues,* Vol. III, Nos. 1 and 2, 1951, pp. 1–34.
45 Lewis Mumford, *The Urban Prospect* (London: Secker & Warburg, 1968), especially Chapter 2, "Planning for the Phases of Life," originally published in 1949.
46 George C. Homans, "Bringing Men Back In," *American Sociological Review,* Vol. 29, No. 6, December 1964, pp. 809–818, and *The Nature of Social Science* (New York: Harcourt, Brace & World, 1967).

simply by not picking up waiting passengers. An inspector stopped him along his route: "That's the only reason you're out on the road, you know." How can we find our way back to such a simple reason for a field whose original validity lies in providing space and shelter for the individual's behavior?

Herbert Gans has been the foremost discussant within sociology and city planning of the limitations to the strength of the environment's influence on the quality of social life. He has enriched the planner's outlook with concepts such as the potential and the effective environment, with empirical research on working-class families in suburbia, with participant observation documentation of ethnic groups' use of physical space in cities. Suzanne Keller has reviewed exhaustively and synthesized such sociological literature as exists on the mainstay of the planner's conceptual armature, the neighborhood.[47] Robert Gutman is following sociology's role in the culture of architecture and studying the actors in the design process as a participant.[48] Robert Sommer is also participating in the designer's work both as a pure researcher in psychology and as friendly critic.[49] Each of them, and others pursuing related lines of inquiry, has drawn distinctions about physical facts and their limited consequences, documented the influence of the designer's personal norms and values, analyzed the use made by inhabitants of the environment in contrast to the designer's intentions—all this in a readily available literature. What has not yet been stated is a way of regularizing the infusion of their findings, insights, and research capabilities into the designing process while it is going on, so as to influence its consequences. As things are now, neither the theory behind nor the procedures for creating new environments affords an essential or persuasive place for human scientists at the time plans are being drawn. And so the problem I have set myself is to suggest some concepts that may help us to put these contributions to work within a process not only under the control of others, but one without a theoretical point of view of its own.

Environment and Behavior: Defining the Problem

Current research by both human scientists and environmental designers ranges farther, wider, and deeper than ever before,

[47] Keller, *The Urban Neighborhood.*
[48] See the Bibliography for a complete list of papers by Robert Gutman.
[49] Robert Sommer, *Personal Space: The Behavioral Basis of Design* (Englewood Cliffs: Prentice-Hall, 1969).

and as in any developing area, investigators seem overly involved in bits and pieces, unrelated and unsynthesized.[50] The prior task of problem-definition has received less attention than it needs.[51]

The Traditional Experimental Model in Design. Research into the "effect of the physical environment on behavior" pursued according to the standards of natural science will codify a wide range of response levels of the human mind and body to a variety of physical conditions.[52] Though the space and underwater programs have accelerated this work, developing the tools

[50] The *Directory of Behavior and Environmental Design,* the third edition of which was published in 1969, lists "persons practicing the various disciplines which deal with the relationships between human behavior and environmental design"—numbering two hundred fifty in thirty-four fields (Research and Design Institute, P.O. Box 307, Providence, Rhode Island). *Man-Environment Systems* is a subscription publication of bibliography, conference summaries, and research abstracts, published six times a year (S-126 Human Development, University Park, Pennsylvania). The Environmental Design Research Association has published the proceedings of its first annual conference, *EDRA I,* edited by Henry Sanoff and Sidney Cohn (School of Design, North Carolina State University, Raleigh, 1970).

[51] Besides Robert Gutman and Robert Sommer, some others giving attention to problem-definition per se are: Kenneth H. Craik, "The Prospects for an Environmental Psychology," IPAR Research Bulletin, University of California Institute of Personality Assessment and Research, 1966, mimeo; Janet Daley, "Psychological Research in Architecture: The Myth of Quantifiability," *The Architects' Journal,* 21 August 1968, pp. 339–341; David C. Glass and Jerome E. Singer, "Social Psychological Reactions to Complex Stressors—Research Prospectus," September 1968, 70 pp., mimeo. (Glass is at Rockefeller University, New York City and Singer is at the State University of New York, Stony Brook.); F. J. Langdon, "The Social and Physical Environment: A Social Scientist's View," Building Research Station, Current Papers, Design Series 61; Brian Wells, "Toward a Definition of Environmental Studies: A Psychologist's Contribution," *The Architects' Journal,* 22 September 1965, pp. 677–683.

[52] "[These publications] serve to highlight the fact that very little is known about the impact of the total environment on learning in particular or on human behavior in general. Curiously enough, the problem of human requirements has had no serious research attention until recently as a basis for determining the design of buildings. . . . As a result there is a dearth of scientifically grounded information concerning the effects man-contrived environments are likely to have on their occupants." C. Theodore Larson, Director, School Environments Research Project, in *SER 3: Environmental Analysis.* Other publications of the series are: *SER 1: Environmental Abstracts* and *SER 2: Environmental Evaluations* (Ann Arbor: University of Michigan, 1965). These articles, for example, in *SER 2,* can be said to stand as comprehensive reviews, but so-called "definitive works" have yet to be written: Daniel H. Carson, "The Interactions of Man and His Environment," pp. 13–50; Joseph R. Akerman, "The Thermally Related Environment and Its Effect on Man," pp. 73–98; Robert A. Boyd, "The Luminous Environment and Its Effects on Man," pp. 101–131; Norman E. Barnett and Bruce E. Erickson, "The Sonic Environment and Its Effects on Man," pp. 133–155.

of measurement and constructing valid experiments will still occupy hundreds of lifetimes, and in the doing much is likely to be uncovered about basic life processes. The single-variable, cause-and-effect model is a welcome discipline for the strictly intuitive understandings so traditional to design. But whether it should be the only model, or indeed, the dominant one, is a question the environment-and-behavior field needs to keep open. Sommer expresses discomfort about the meaning of some of his work in these terms, suggesting that it is not the "rule" that his type of research can deliver, but instead the kinds of things that can be found out about and formed into a context the designer can make use of.[53]

The pursuit of pseudoproblems is a growing source of unease to designers and human scientists alike, as questions are bent to conform to the model.[54] At the extreme, Studer has attempted to turn the behavioral technology of Skinner into an operational equation for stating the effect of environment on behavior, expecting to achieve a quantifiable and predictable relationship: "an environmental configuration which will produce, with the highest probability, the specified state of behavioral events. What this clearly describes is . . . the acquisition of, or modification toward, a new system of behaviors. . . ."[55] Again, the model as Studer explains it clarifies thought-processes beneficial to intui-

[53] Sommer, *Personal Space,* p. 11.
[54] "In the present stage of our knowledge, human behavior is often seen as the outcome of the joint working of a number of distinct and often unrelated factors. . . . Consequently, two-variable causal laws are often inadequate, and important magnitudes are not scalable. In a sense, we know too much to be able to unify it in a single theory, and we do not know any of it with sufficient sureness. The problem of combining factors is not automatically solved by formulating the combination in terms of a field theory. We do not obtain such a theory merely by recognizing a multiplicity of factors and treating them as constituting a phase space, as Lewin has pointed out. How the factors combine in their working must still be specified. . . . We need to know, not only the separate factors that are determinative of behavior, but also how they interact with one another. It is not always possible to advance step by step; to arrive at a good theory may call for as much boldness as imagination." Abraham Kaplan, *The Conduct of Inquiry: Methodology for Behavioral Science* (San Francisco: Chandler Publishing Company, 1964), pp. 325–326.
[55] Raymond G. Studer, "The Dynamics of Behavior-Contingent Physical Systems," paper presented at the Symposium on Design Methods, Portsmouth College of Technology (England), December 1967, pp. 14, 15, 18. Studer has also called, as I am here, for a "syntactical glue for continuity between the physical and the behavioral" in *Socio-Physical Technology* (Proceedings of the 2nd Annual Workshop in Socio-Physical Technology) (Washington: American Institute of Architects, 1970), p. 35.

tion, but the vocabulary is replete with certainties that can never be achieved.

The experimental model does assure the delineation of gross effects—where the physical situation is gross and the human response is as well. Overcrowding, isolation, loud noises, floods, dim light, traffic jams—all have very nearly visible or readily measurable human response levels. But usually, in the process of designing an environment, gross effects, if looked for, are relatively easy to foresee. Previous experience with similar conditions may be the only data needed, and ordinary common sense may be capable of estimating even quite complicated repercussions. Finely calibrated effects, as in concert halls, can be simulated. The effects not anticipated and not intended are those that bring difficulties over time, and they are likely to occur at the subtle end of the range. There are also more of them, and intuitive empathy may not be adequate for perceiving them. They are unobtrusive enough to be dismissed by the designer's biases, cultural and intellectual. But these subtle and qualitative relationships between environment and behavior are now beginning to interest us, especially at the time of creating a new environment. Glass and Singer have posed their research into urban stressors in just these terms, by measuring the *delayed* effect of acoustic stress on task effectiveness and frustration tolerance—the extent of the costs of adaptation subsequent to the immediate experience.[56] The quantifying model, enabling us to state statistically the limits of human adaptation as a function of the physical environment, should, however, be complemented with an ethology of human adaptation in the urban environment—that is, qualitative descriptions of the kinds of adaptive behaviors people use, besides deviance; as in animal ethology, the search for causes best comes only after complete description.[57] These adaptive human behaviors are the very stuff

[56] "The review papers just discussed leave one critical question unanswered: Granting that noise does not generally affect behavior adversely, and that in the long-run the organism can adapt to aversive sound, to what extent does the adaptation produce after-effects detectable in behavior? It is possible that psychophysiological responses to a complex stressor like noise become adapted to it, yet important after-effects remain in the form of lowered tolerance for frustration and heightened irritability." Glass and Singer, "Social Psychological Reactions to Complex Stressors," pp. 5–6.

[57] "The major premise of ethology is that the study of animal behavior must begin by obtaining as complete a knowledge as possible on the behavior of the species in question during the entire life cycle. A collection of such observations on one species is called an ethogram. It simply describes what an animal does, not why it does it. . . . After the different behaviors have

of "diversity," and some of them are, as Dubos warns, also likely to be used to screen out alternative ways of behaving in the future.[58] Beyond the extremes of pathological behavior, the descriptive literature is scanty. We have no way of evaluating the healthfulness of adaptations unless we can compare them over time in similar populations.

The kind of adaptation deplored by moral philosophers of environment seems to be "habituation"—the numbing of the sensibilities to ugliness, to banality, to dulling repetition, to pollution, to discordant noise. But somehow designers seem to adopt a frame of mind that excludes adaptation and habituation from the original definition of the situation, and so the "effect of environment on people" is presumed to have the great impact and strong reaction of a first encounter—each time. The interaction is perceived as immediate, mainly visual, and not repeated. What happens after the novelty wears off is not a concern. The scarcity of a research literature in architecture that evaluates environments in use may have its source in the unexamined belief that human behaviors are transitory, unsustained, nonrepetitive, and not habit-forming—a view of people as largely impulse-ridden. Human anxiety can be relieved by discharging impulses for immediate gratification, but it is also handled by being surrounded with things one is sure of: the customs of the group, the familiar place, and the beaten path. The built environment as a whole is insufficiently studied for information about the rate of cultural change, but in the absence of data, the presumption in architecture has been that it is rapid—which may have more to do with short-lived fads and evolving styles in the culture of architecture than with the characteristics of people.[59]

been classified and compared, the next step is their analysis in the light of the factors entering into or influencing these behaviors. A study is made of the probable evolution, ontogenetic development, survival value or function, and the physiological bases of these behaviors." Eckhard H. Hess, "Ethology: An Approach Toward the Complete Analysis of Behavior," in *New Directions in Psychology* (New York: Holt, Rinehart and Winston, 1962), pp. 159–160.

58 René Dubos, "Environmental Determinants of Human Life," in *Environmental Influences*, David C. Glass, editor (New York: Rockefeller University Press and Russell Sage Foundation, 1968), pp. 138–154.

59 "Novelty, which has been considered a major characteristic of architecture, is in fact *atypical* of most primitive and vernacular buildings, and is a culturally linked phenomenon of recent vintage." Amos Rapoport, *House Form and Culture* (Englewood Cliffs, N. J.: Prentice-Hall, 1969) p. 12. See also Rapoport's discussion of "Constancy and Change," pp. 78–82.

The fallacy of an "environmental determinism" of behavior is increasingly acknowledged on all sides and the intervening variables are accorded the respect due them, even if they are never analyzed. But the pressure remains for the designer to foresee the consequences, insofar as he can, of what he creates—and so we are pushed full circle, back to the kinds of truths the experimental model can deliver. In this, a lingering presumption of the dominance of physical objects over behavior controls the formulation of research questions, and yet it seems to me that no theoretical outlook in environmental design can exist at much remove from either human events or human purposes. Sommer's reports of the ways in which people arrange themselves at library tables when they do not want to be distracted are more a description and explanation of human response in an interpersonal situation than an approach to a "theory of chair arrangements."[60] A studio class of mine was assigned drawing tables in a large space also occupied by other studio classes. But when the class on occasion was held as a seminar instead of under individual tutelage, the space reverberated too much for give-and-take among ten people, so we moved into a regular classroom for those sessions. The studio space expresses the norms of the culture of architectural education, where students are expected to talk freely in small groups, to see each other's work, perhaps to listen to music as they draw, all because they are expected to put in a great deal of time at their drawing boards—unlike students in other fields whose time is spent more in solitude reading or writing. Our seminar meetings were not in this pattern, and did not belong to the architect's original intentions for the space he created; and so to carry out *our* intentions we had to move to a classroom. Had we stayed in the studio, holding our seminar in a space not intended for it, we would have expressed adaptive behaviors under the headings of human frustration, interpersonal communication, small group dynamics, cognition —all kinds of human events and not a "theory of spaces."

The physical environment is said to influence social and interpersonal relationships, leading the planner to believe he can maximize human interaction with a particular site plan or building arrangement. Environments may be criticized when they "keep people apart." The location of furniture is said to influence or control interpersonal relationships. In ordinary

60 Sommer, *Personal Space,* pp. 54–57.

parlance the place or the room is said to "just make people" behave as they do. That social and interpersonal relationships are always a concomitant of spatial arrangements and physical elements is hardly a fact to be received with surprise. Their *quality*, however, is so much more a function of nonspatial and nonphysical variables that research in environmental design to predict that quality is misguided. In a study of the effects of a "beautiful" and an "ugly" room on the mood and perception of subjects and on their evaluation of a psychiatrist, though a significant difference in the perception of each kind of room was found, no "simple environmental effects" showed, and further, the findings "strongly suggest that potential environmental effects on interpersonal perception depend on the personality characteristics considered."[61]

Relating is neutral and not much of a goal when we realize how many ways of relating there are. Proximity, for example, can mean conflict or intimacy between people, and even though society may value intimacy over conflict, there is no basis for valuing proximity over distance in psychological terms alone.[62] There may be justification in design terms for clustering housing together in order to economize on utility connections, but to consider a "proximity" born of technical and financial objectives as "intimacy" in psychological terms is meaningless. Being able to "see" other people—in a neighborhood, in an office corridor —is only the opportunity for interpersonal relations. Whether and where to provide that opportunity as well as the equally valid opportunity for privacy and nonrelating is a *data question*, not a conceptual one, to be answered by the values and priorities of the inhabitants. Without such data the design may provide each kind of opportunity just where it turns out to be least consonant with the inhabitants' values—as in the Pruitt-Igoe public housing project where the residents' fear of one another led them to value a secure and adequate dwelling over and above the chance meetings and group socializing the building was

61 Joyce V. Kasmar, William V. Griffin, and Joseph H. Mauritzen, "The Effect of Environmental Surroundings on Outpatients' Mood and Perception of Psychiatrists," *Journal of Consulting and Clinical Psychology*, Vol. 32, No. 2, April 1968, pp. 223–226.
62 "Those who subscribe to architectural determinism always seem to suppose that the influence of design will be beneficial. But people may be rancorous as well as friendly, and, as several studies of neighbouring families have shown, they may equally well wish to defend themselves against their neighbours as to welcome every opportunity to meet them." Broady, *Planning for People*, pp. 18–19.

designed to maximize.[63] On the other hand, examples abound of isolated subdivisions where young mothers want more adult relationships than there is opportunity for.

The ways in which "environmental influences *on* interpersonal behavior" are commonly conceived lead to a view of people as passive—the "dependent" variable in more ways than one. When we change the location of the chair in order to make conversation possible or less of an auditory strain, we have influenced the environment, not the other way round. But, it may be countered, if the chair were located correctly in the first place, moving it would not be necessary—and so the environment is the cause of the behavior of moving the chair. The assumption of such utter disjunction between people and objects at this scale is an absurdity—are people observably so passive toward objects and ignorant of their own purposes? The behavior of conversing is inextricably tied to the capability for doing so, and that capability may be mediated through an object (chairs side by side or a telephone) or through adaptive behavior (shouting or writing letters). What is deplorable, however, is that predicting what chair location "will do to" conversation is made into a question that supposedly can be generalized about as a result of experiment—and these have often been made either with physically and mentally disabled subjects or with people under the control of a single set of institutional rules. The single-variable experimental model can hope only to establish one kind of physical arrangement or another as the independent variable leading to particular human consequences in conditions where human purposes are exactly the same.

The methods of the biological sciences, particularly animal biology and ecology, which rely heavily upon observation and field experimentation over long periods, seem more applicable to the design fields than the single variable laboratory experiments characteristic of physics and chemistry. A designer would profit more from training in the techniques of systematic observation than in the empty rituals included under the category of experimental design.[64]

What we abhor most in the environment is precisely the use of formula, as it were, to prescribe uniform, undifferentiated, stereotyped, and insensitive environments for what is the essential human condition of diversity, growth, and autonomy. The lack

[63] Lee Rainwater, "Fear and the House-As-Haven in the Lower Class," *Journal of the American Institute of Planners*, Vol. 32, No. 1, January 1966, p. 29.

[64] Sommer, *Personal Space*, p. 166.

of a theory of human nature for environmental design is felt most of all on this issue.

Human Nature and Visual Perception. The outlook today coming closest to a theory of human nature for environmental design is embodied in perception: the variables that mediate between the person and the external world are visual, leading to moods, preferences, directional orientation, learning, aesthetic pleasure. What people see and what it means to them is not the simple question it appears; but because it is the shared reference point for the experience of environment, the search for meaning—for laymen as well as scientists and designers—begins there. Human perceptual and cognitive attributes have always interested psychologists and environmental designers have been a natural audience for their concepts and research.[65] Whether they can put them to use is only one side of the question: how do the creations of the designer extend the understandings of the psychologist about the workings of the mind?

One reason psychological research into perception and environmental meaning is so important is that many myths about cause and effect need to be denied or confirmed. Physical arrangements in the environment are described, quite reasonably, as "open, closed, free, flexible, ordered, harmonious, delightful, communicating, relating, inviting, welcoming," and so on. However, used by designers to explain their intentions toward people, such terms are used also to project an interior state of mind or purpose. People are described as "cut off" from each other because a fence cuts off one land area from another. Of a house standing alone, the designer might say, "Now, to decrease the isolation of this family . . . ." What qualities *do* go to make up a family's isolation? Of a group of row houses that are all alike, the critic will say, "See how monotonous this makes community life!" What *are* the characteristics of monotonous community life? "Ease of access," often a goal in designing roads and paths in sites and neighborhoods, is seen simultaneously as the way people will feel toward each other when they live there.

65 See, for example, an extensive bibliography in Kenneth H. Craik, "Human Responsiveness to Landscape: An Environmental Psychological Perspective," Institute of Personality Assessment and Research, University of California, Berkeley, pp. 18–22; and the discussion "Perception" and "Symbolization," in Christian Norberg-Schulz, *Intentions in Architecture* (Cambridge: M.I.T. Press, 1965), pp. 27–82.

Ruskin defined the "pathetic fallacy" as any metaphorical statement which endows an inanimate object with the power to feel
and act,[66] or, as Fowler has it, "the tendency to credit nature
with human emotions."[67] A habit of speech in environmental
design attributes animate qualities to physical objects and
anthropomorphizes them. But streets and spaces are "dead or
alive" by virtue of their human use (the schedule of buses, the
zoning classification, the collection of garbage), not by virtue of
their scenic properties. The "gaiety" of bright colors—a staple of
cosmetic urban improvement—on brick walls, trash cans, store-
fronts, and kiosks evokes an especial gloom when bad conditions otherwise and underneath stay the same.

Visual meanings may or may not be affective meanings in direct
translation. The feelings people have are in a different realm
from the physical environment; the plan which has connected-
ness and order within itself, for its own reasons, does not carry
those same meanings into the affective realm. Such a plan might
be experienced as affirming a person's feelings of belonging,
where they already exist; but certainly alienation also can persist
in a person in a neighborhood whose design expresses harmony
and accessibility in physical terms.

The historical European reasons for the plaza—as the sole
source of water, as the marshaling yard for baroque ceremonials
—do not exist within urbanized society. Yet designers and critics
will demand a plaza "in order to create a sense of community"
—and so we make large commitments of public funds to per-
petuate yet another pathetic fallacy in design. We have not
faced the reasons why most public open space gets relatively
little use, and if we were to, then we would have to begin an
anthropological and sociological inquiry into leisure activities,
the components of morale and consensus, shopping, car use,
kinship patterns, and the changing role of women in the work
force. But the pathetic fallacy here has led us away from the
kinds of public policy that might indeed help to fulfill the
human need for a sense of community: much larger indoor
living space for small-group meetings; a huge increase in invest-

66 John Ruskin, "Of the Pathetic Fallacy (*Modern Painters,* Vol. III, pt. 4),"
in *The Great Critics: An Anthology of Literary Criticism,* edited by Smith
and Parks (New York: W. W. Norton & Company, 1939), pp. 723–727.
67 "*Sphinxlike, siren-sweet, sly, benign, impassive, vindictive, callously in-
different the sea may seem to a consciousness addicted to pathetic fallacies.*"
H. W. Fowler, *A Dictionary of Modern English Usage* (London: Oxford University Press, 1952), p. 426.

ment in public television; more stoops; free postage and telephones; new public holidays and rituals.

Perception as the mediating variable between environmental design and its human consequences is, I am suggesting, of limited help in explaining a relationship between human nature and environment. In a study of residents of public housing, only 8 percent of the respondents "made any references to a nonpractical, aesthetic quality of the house; the remainder were concerned with the ease of cleaning, convenient room sizes, good storage facilities, and so on."[68] And a study of tenants in a Scottish housing project "found that tenants . . . noticed and complained about practical things, such as the lack of made-up footpaths, but failed to remark upon the unsightly colliery slagheaps or the monotonous appearance of their houses. Indeed, in another estate, they even failed to distinguish between an older and a more modern style of housing."[69] In a study of whether the intentions of the architect with regard to the visual and formal qualities of buildings were received as such by laymen, not only were about half the judgments significantly different, but they went in opposite directions: "[the architects] would judge a building to be good, pleasing, beautiful, interesting, exciting, and unique; the Non-architects would judge it to be bad, annoying, ugly, boring, calming, and common."[70] Differences in sophistication and taste are complex, and I do not mean to lay any burden upon them, but such findings as these contain the germs of new ideas about the relationship between human nature and the physical environment, to which attention must be paid. There is no discounting the joys and benefits human nature reaps in contact with beauty of all kinds. But we can no longer leave it at the satisfying look of things: the satisfactions have also got to come from daily pleasure in use.

Another Formulation to Guide Research. The concept of stimulus-response is also widely used for conceiving the relation between environment and behavior: What kind and level of stimulus does an object present to a person as evidenced in his response? But as used in environmental design, the model gives discouraging results in pinpointing the source of the stimulus for the

[68] Cooper, "Some Social Implications of House and Site Plan Design," p. 35.
[69] Broady, *Planning for People,* p. 21.
[70] Robert G. Hershberger, "A Study of Meaning and Architecture," paper presented at the First Annual Conference of the Environmental Design Research Association, Chapel Hill, North Carolina, June 1969, pp. 29 and 32.

particular behavioral result observed.[71] Even more than its methodological limitations for environmental design, the very independence of the person from the constraints of the physical environment should enforce upon us a methodology more appropriate to what is being measured. He expresses this independence by various forms of self-adaptation at varying amounts of cost in energy, in time, in life-span, in money, in self-esteem, in physical health. He also adapts the environment to express his values, and when these adaptations are not beneficial to the largest number over the long run, they become—like air pollution and strip mining—social costs.

I propose that what we have described as the effect of environment on behavior is actually *the extent to which the environment responds to the stimulus of human demands,* so that the adaptations people make are the measure of the appropriateness of a physical response. Adaptations will be found on a range of less to more intense, costly, or deviant. The success of environmental responses in meeting human purposes can be evaluated according to the human adaptations observed: the physical resources for behavior can be undermining to supportive, absent to present, rare to ubiquituous. Human purposes in turn have definable characteristics that evoke environmental responses, ranging from specific to general. Thus the two ends of the environmental response continuum are *structured, directive, and authoritarian,* on the one hand, and *minimal, open,* and *flexible,* on the other. A middle term, which is the one responded with least often, is *congruent.*

Structured, directive, and authoritarian environments charge a high adaptive cost which people, when they are willing, pay because the consequences are rewarding. The concert will be pleasing, so people will sit still in row upon row and not be frustrated at a narrow choice of behaviors. Jails, street patterns and traffic lights, rooms with teaching machines, hospitals, telephone booths, capsules traveling to the moon—all these are physical responses to human behaviors having limited or specific purposes. The narrow range of behavior may be the purpose of a social institution, as in jails where the environment defines a negation of behaviors. When we question a building for its highly structured environment, we are likely to be questioning

71 William V. Griffin, Joseph H. Mauritzen, Joyce V. Kasmar, "The Psychological Aspects of the Architectural Environment: A Review," *American Journal of Psychiatry,* Vol. 25, No. 8, February 1969, pp. 1057–1062.

the institution and its purposes: when the social institution of a free public education shared an unquestioned understanding of its aims and methods, school buildings could come stamped out of a mold; now the environmental response, of moveable walls and dual-purpose spaces, has its source in the questions being asked about how learning happens. But not all limited and specific human purposes represent negations or punishments: the closest approximations so far to a theory of human nature for environmental design have been in responses to the *absence* of behaviors, that is, people with behavioral disabilities or inabilities are compensated by their physical environment: hospitals, training facilities, housing for the elderly, facilities for the handicapped are built on the assumption that the physical environment can be a specific or prosthetic resource for many kinds of behavior.[72]

A variant of the structured, directive, and authoritarian environment is the *captive environment*, where the consequences are not rewarding and the adaptation unhealthful—air and water pollution, traffic jams, defaced landscapes, slums. No immediate control over these environments is possible: they neither respond to human purposes nor allow a person, no matter how active, to modify them, partly because the controlling conditions are usually diffuse and complex. Pointing out captive environments is a widespread kind of social criticism. "Wishful" architectural determinism is what designers often suffer the delusion of, when they assume one consequence and reality delivers another—permanent, unyielding, and captive. An especially distasteful environment of this kind is one designed for an indirectly affected group of users—in schools, for example, where maintenance men are taken into account over and above the students and teachers; and in playgrounds, "an administrator's heaven and a child's hell."[73]

Minimally articulated, open, and flexible environments charge a low adaptive cost because people can create the physical

72 Selwyn Goldsmith, *Designing for the Disabled: A Manual of Technical Information* (London: RIBA Technical Information Service, 1963); M. Powell Lawton, "Planning Environments for Older People," *Journal of the American Institute of Planners,* Vol. 36, No. 2, March 1970, pp. 124–129; Ogden R. Lindsley, "Geriatric Behavioral Prosthetics," in Robert Kastenbaum, editor, *New Thoughts on Old Age* (New York: Springer Publishing Company, 1964), pp. 41–60; Bertram Berenson, "Sensory Architecture," *Landscape,* Vol. 17, No. 2, Winter 1967–68, pp. 19–21.

73 Sommer, *Personal Space,* p. 79.

response to suit their own behaviors and purposes, reducing their frustrations directly and fulfilling their own needs. Camping grounds, dual-purpose rooms with moveable dividers, squatter housing and other indigenous architecture, people's parks—all are physical responses that accept change readily. Glass and Singer have included in their hypotheses the possibility that individual control over the source of acoustic stress reduces its psychic cost, and their findings have shown just that.[74] But open and flexible environments should be a positive response by the designer, not one representing his indecision. The indeterminate future is the source of considerable anxiety among designers, and it is the reason they offer for indeterminate architecture. But the indeterminacy of the future, which we all have in common, may turn out to be an inadequate determination of the behaviors people can be discovered to have and to value. Relying on man to bear the costs of adaptation, rather than trying to meet him as he is, has brought us to the present pass.

Contemporary alienation from and frustration with the physical environment stem, in these terms, from authoritarian environments imposed on human purposes that really require a diversity of spaces and places in order to be carried out without unwanted adaptive cost. Overly unarticulated environments, at the other extreme, fail to accommodate the full range of purposes—the office bullpen where private conversation is impossible or the "open space" for "free" play that can never include basketball or tennis. A *congruent* environmental response is lacking. Office buildings and mass housing are two examples today where such anomalies persist in the face of demonstrable displeasure, discomfort, and obliteration of human individuality. They run the gamut from rabbit warrens to circus tents. A building can be congruent with the kind of life to go on in it, and at the same time be tied down to details of electricity, elevators, plumbing. But a congruent environmental response is not a "package plan." It is instead a plan that uses the behaviors of the future inhabitants as the imperatives of design.

As more persons find the opportunity to express their biological endowment under diversified conditions, society becomes richer and civilizations continue to unfold. In contrast, if the surroundings and ways of life are highly stereotyped, the only components of man's nature that flourish are those adapted to the narrow

[74] David C. Glass, Jerome E. Singer, and Lucy N. Friedman, "Psychic Cost of Adaptation to an Environmental Stressor," *Journal of Personality and Social Psychology*, Vol. 12, No. 3, July 1969, pp. 200–210.

range of prevailing conditions. Hence the dangers of many modern housing developments, which, although sanitary, are inimical to the development of human potentialities and are designed as if their only function was to provide disposable cubicles for dispensable people . . . irrespective of genetic constitution, most young people raised in a featureless environment and limited to a narrow range of life experiences will be crippled intellectually and emotionally.[75]

Observing and recording the diverse adaptations people make, as suggested earlier, does not imply that there is some comfortable middle ground with statable norms already defined. Adaptation is perhaps best thought of as a metaphor for a myriad of processes—physiological, cultural, interpersonal, intrapsychic—happening constantly, and in fact constituting the very subject matter of each social and behavioral science. But to specify the adaptations people do make is not to engage in metaphor. Instead it provides the likelihood of bringing into the heart of environmental design the empirical data and methods of the human sciences as an authentic collaboration. But in order to particularize the relationship between what people do and the physical environment in which they do it, the diverse adaptations people can be seen to have need to be tied to some way of understanding what they do and do not get out of making them. Each of the human sciences also tries to find that out: each has concepts around which they fit their data on the operational and functional outcomes of whatever adaptive process they are studying—concepts such as species survival, homeostasis, secondary gain, frustration, cognitive dissonance.

The concept environmental design might organize its data around, as it measures and estimates the consequences of what it does and proposes to do, is that of the *sense of competence* people have in carrying out their everyday behavior—visiting, working, playing, learning, shopping, meditating, cooking. The central source of data is people's own evaluation of their sense of competence and objective measures of it, relative to the availability, extent, quality, and placement of environmental resources. The very process of design is, then, to be conceived as a response to the stimuli of human demands: the object in the environment is not lying there waiting for its stimulus properties to take effect upon the person, but instead the person endows the object with various kinds of stimulus properties depending

75 Dubos, "Environmental Determinants of Human Life," pp. 153–154.

upon the extent to which he can carry out effective behavior that uses the object as a resource. What is considered effective behavior varies among people as a function of age, culture, education; and so competence has to be measured relatively. The stimulus properties of environment—its variable meanings—arise from these differences.

The general notion of "interaction" with the environment subsumes too much and needs this tighter specification of consequences. Even so, what I narrow down to is still very wide: self-esteem, morale, independence, previous experiences, learning capacity, birth position—any number of additional psychological and situational variables intervene in the measurement of the sense of competence. But I do intend that measures of the sense of competence replace measures of preference, because what people "prefer" may obscure the details of what people gain their level of competence and effectiveness from. And they are details with which environmental design can realistically deal effectively.

What this leads to is measuring the stress and strain of adaptation in the physical environment in terms of ego strength, just as physiologic stress is measured with heart rate and blood pressure. White originated the concept of a sense of competence in psychoanalytic theory because a complete theory of personality could not be achieved unless "the facts of exploration, manipulation, locomotion, language, the practicing of motor skills, the growth of cognition, the development of plans and intentional actions, and the emergence of higher thought processes" are seen as the "growth processes whereby man's complex repertory of adaptive behavior comes to be put together."[76] Where environmental design enters, then, is in the concrete reality White acknowledges the ego handling—gaining or losing strength from the encounter:

Effectance is a prompting to explore the properties of the environment; it leads to an accumulating knowledge of what can and cannot be done with the environment; its biological significance lies in this very property of developing *competence*. Instinctual energies likewise produce action, effects, and knowledge of the environment, thus making a contribution to competence. But their contribution is necessarily narrower than that of neutral energies which stand ever ready to promote exploration for its own sake. . . . Competence is the cumulative result of the history of interactions with the environment. *Sense of competence* is suggested as a suitable term for the subjective side of this, signifying one's consciously or unconsciously felt competence—one's confidence—in dealing with the various aspects of the environment. It is easier to describe these concepts in transactions with inanimate objects, but they apply equally well, and more importantly, to interactions with other human beings. Human objects present the same problem of finding out what can and cannot be done with them . . . and we can assume that great importance will always be attached to one's *sense of interpersonal competence.*[77]

One thread running through such environment-and-behavior literature as there is, is that social and interpersonal interaction is the most important kind of behavior tied to the environment. Interpersonal competence is certainly one manifestation of competence, but only one. Given the limited importance of the physical environment to the quality of interpersonal relations, the content of the adaptations people make in order to maintain their sense of competence relative to the physical environment may best be found elsewhere. Two kinds of adaptations come to mind: the substitutions people make of one behavior for another, and the enacted "defense mechanisms" people use to establish their dominance over—or competence to deal with— threatening situations. When the walk to the grocery store is very long and there is no bus to take, does the tired housewife prepare meals below a certain nutrition level? When storage space in the kitchen is too limited to permit saving money by buying large quantities at lower cost, what other life activities are given up? What is the relation between various kinds of property ownership and the sense of competence for different groups? Public housing tenants receiving welfare in Chicago are known to have as many as three telephones in the same apartment: What is given up in order to pay for symbolic self-esteem? How are various environmental elements (fences, cars, lawns) used to minimize interactions with others viewed as threatening, as a definition of "territory?"[78]

---

[77] Ibid., pp. 185–186. A strong relationship among physical movement, competence, and ego strength is discussed in Jarl E. Dyrud and Charles Donnelly, "Executive Functions of the Ego—Clinical and Procedural Relevance," *Archives of General Psychiatry*, Vol. 20, March 1969, pp. 257–261.

[78] "Aggression in animals rarely occurs in pure form; it is only one of two components of an adaptive system. This is most clearly seen in territorial behavior, although it is also true of most other types of hostile behavior. Members of territorial species divide, among themselves, the available living space and opportunities by each individual defending its home range against competitors. Now in this system of parceling out living space, avoidance plays as important a part as attack . . ." N. Tinbergen, "On War and Peace in Animals and Man," *Science*, Vol. 160, 28 June 1968, p. 1417.

The Baltimore housing study by Wilner and others posed several hypotheses along these lines. Self-esteem and morale were measured in subjects who had lived in an improved physical environment for a while, but the questions were of a general nature having no specific connections with the different environment. The research assumed that general attitudes are simply permeated by the physical surroundings. The attitudes measured fall into the category of "world-view," and the results showed no convincing differences between the better-housed group and the group still in the ghetto (in fact, each group showed an advance in "healthier" outlook during the years of the study).[79] If the scales had been constructed using the physical environment as the basis of specific competencies in, say, studying or cooking or the whole daily round, learning what other attitudes were simultaneously affected, then the research would at least have tested what the hypotheses stated. There is a useful and crucial difference between *being* in an environment and *doing things in it*. White has said the same thing in elaborating his concept:

[Experiments are reported] in which children of different ages brought back from places such as a canal dock or a department store entirely different descriptions depending upon what they had found to do in these locations.

The objective stable world is thus best conceived of as a construction based upon action. Knowledge about the environment is knowledge of the probable consequences of action. It is a system of readinesses for action which can properly be conceived of as patterns of facilitation and inhibition in the nervous system. This is the form in which reality leaves its record.[80]

A pilot study by Schooler of four thousand elderly persons sixty-five and over, not institutionalized, is an instance in a different vein of research that might be able to explain more than it does if the concept of the sense of competence vis-à-vis the physical environment were introduced. The study sought to establish the relation between the characteristics of the residential environment, social behavior, and the emotional and physical health of the elderly, hoping to work toward "a theory of the aging process which recognized the organic or interactive nature of the environment in affecting the eventual success of the individual's adaptation to the aging process . . . [the hypothesis is that] environmental characteristics affect successful adaptation

[79] Wilner et al. *The Housing Environment*, pp. 201–212, 275–278, and 329–334.
[80] White, "Ego and Reality," p. 188.

to aging as reflected in the older person's morale, but this effect is mediated through the formation and maintenance of social relationships which themselves are to some extent determined by the various characteristics of the environment."[81] The findings show that "the relation between morale and social relations is . . . not much to begin with, but it is even less when environmental factors are controlled for."[82] I would like to see a hypothesis tested that sustains the relationship between environmental characteristics and morale, but mediated by the person's sense of competence in carrying out various purposes and behaviors, *only one of which is socializing.* Competence in social interaction may sensibly be postulated to have peaks and valleys of priority throughout the life cycle, with other forms of behavior affording more reward to a sense of competence at different times. For the aged, their competence may be reflected in independent gross motor activity, cooking without breaking dishes or spilling food, bathing in comfort without fear of slipping or miscalculating, doing housework without accidents— everyday events in which the physical environment is primary. Schooler concludes that the data force the hypothesis that environmental factors are more significant to morale than social relations, and the mediating term he suggests be tested next is simply perceptual and cognitive appreciation of the environment.[83]

Another study tested "the assertion that better housing can be used as a tool for raising the productivity and improving the health of workers in less developed countries."[84] Worker absenteeism and the number of visits to a free outpatient clinic were used as the variables whose rates should change as the sample population lived in higher quality (new) housing. With the exception of the elimination of rats, "none of 13 other variables representing changes in various aspects of housing quality was significantly related to changes in outpatient visits," and the use

81 Kermit K. Schooler, "On The Relation Between Characteristics of Residential Environment, Social Behavior, and the Emotional and Physical Health of the Elderly in the United States," paper presented to the Eighth International Congress of Gerontology, Washington, D.C., August 1969, pp. 1–2.

82 Ibid., p. 7.

83 Ibid., p. 8.

84 Robert G. Healy, *Effects of Housing on Health and Productivity (Preliminary),* International Housing Productivity Study; Housing, Real Estate, and Urban Land Studies Program, Graduate School of Business Administration, University of California, Los Angeles, October 1968, p. 1.

of absenteeism was found to be a "relatively poor proxy for more direct measures of health" because it was so dependent upon other variables.[85] But most interestingly, in the first year of living in their new housing, *absenteeism increased 105 percent,* because the workers stayed around home, landscaping and making enclosed patios. Absenteeism dropped to its usual level in the second year. "Loma Jardin residents have devoted themselves enthusiastically to *improving their new homes*"[86] (italics mine). Why should their new homes attract their improvement energies when their former housing, presumably in *need* of improvements, did not? The research does not ask that question, but it seems likely it could be related to a general reinforcement of the workers' sense of competence, as expressed in this new energy toward their new housing, which is, perhaps, perceived as *self-improvement* and not simply as a physical object. Competence in one area reinforces efforts to become competent in others. The study tested several hypotheses to explain the first-year absenteeism—none of them satisfactory to the author, but all couched in the quantitative terms of economic analysis. The relationship between productivity—this was a study of the question of whether industry's investment in improved housing would reap profit—and the level of the population's sense of competence and self-esteem is one that could stand testing at many scales—workbench, kitchen, house, school, neighborhood.

One variation on the theme of competence is that of the perception of one's performance as dependent on skill or chance instead of on one's efforts. Rotter has shown that the "effect of a reinforcement . . . is not . . . a simple stamping-in process but depends on whether or not the person perceives a causal relationship between his own behavior and the reward. . . . When a reinforcement is perceived . . . as following some action of his own but not being entirely contingent upon his action, then, in our culture, it is typically perceived as the result of luck, chance, fate, as under the control of powerful others, or as unpredictable because of the great complexity of the forces surrounding him."[87] In many tests of the use of the "Internal-External Scale," Rotter finds that not only do individuals differ in how they regard the

[85] Ibid., pp. 60–64.

[86] Ibid., p. 42.

[87] Julian B. Rotter, "Generalized Expectancies for Internal Versus External Control of Reinforcement," *Psychological Monographs: General and Applied,* Vol. 80, No. 1, Whole No. 609, 1966, pp. 1.

same situation, but "such generalized expectancies can be measured and are predictive of behavior in a variety of circumstances."[88] Because the scale makes it possible to sort populations according to their view of themselves as more and less in control of their performance and the rewards it brings, it would seem on the face of it to be an essential first step in research assessing "the effect of environment on people." Those who perceive themselves as dependent on luck and fate not only have basically different attitudes but they may make behavioral adaptations quite different from those who feel more in control of the consequences of their behavior.

If "other-directed" man is to be de-emphasized, then we need to look for ways of shifting attention away from what depersonalizes and objectifies him. The concern in the social sciences with role and status, structure and function has too eagerly been misappropriated by environmental designers who see these categories as having neat spatial analogues and a mechanistic complexity their tools can handle. In the context of rising populations and the likelihood of many more people occupying the same square feet of space, satisfactions are going to have to arise within the personal compass, where people can see what they accomplish. A man's own satisfaction with his behavior becomes more important than the satisfaction of others with his behavior. The huge scale of future building, so clearly our destiny, sparks this search for ways of helping people stay in touch with themselves.

[88] Ibid., p. 25.

2

Collaboration Toward
a Theory of Human Nature
for Environmental Design

Introduction

Because it is impossible to subject a theory to all possible tests, philosophers of science, Kuhn says, "do not ask whether a theory has been verified but rather about its probability in the light of the evidence that actually exists."[1] With that criterion in mind different theories are then compared on the basis of their capacity to explain the evidence at hand. When one theory is no longer so compelling as another, it is replaced. It would be satisfying to think that environmental design is on the brink of moving from one paradigm—in Kuhn's terminology a body of accepted theory in science used as the basis for commitment and consensus on research and teaching—to another, with more explanatory probability. Instead environmental design may be only on the brink of achieving its first.

In spite of all the confusion there seems to be one point of agreement: the situation is impossible. Who would defend the chaos of the modern metropolis, the destruction of the landscape through characterless building, or the split in conflicting opinions on basic architectural problems? But the disagreement becomes deep and fundamental as soon as we question whether the "modern" movement in architecture and planning really shows the way out of our muddle. . . . We might not always agree with the common criticism of art and literature, but at least we must acknowledge that it undoubtedly has created an increased respect for these fields. For architecture we hardly find any respect whatsoever, either from the public or from the architects. In discussing architectural matters we rarely achieve anything but a quarrel about what you like and what I like. As soon as the problems go beyond the purely physical functions, the architects are completely lost and fall back upon haphazard improvizations.[2]

In searching for the current body of accepted theory, I am aware of leaping over lifetimes of prophets and poets of architecture and planning, past and present. I am not discussing the history of theories in environmental design, but instead theory's present potency for guiding practice, teaching, and—the newcomer—research. Some practice and teaching are effectively relying on the rhetoric, poetry, creeds, buildings, and city plans of great designers—Le Corbusier, Sullivan, Unwin, Wright, Mies, Stein, Gropius, Sert, Kahn, and members of "Team Ten." But the fact that their partisan aesthetics and social ideologies are not hypotheses for emerging research led Christian Norberg-

[1] Thomas S. Kuhn, *The Structure of Scientific Revolutions* (Chicago: University of Chicago Press, 1962), p. 144.
[2] Christian Norberg-Schulz, *Intentions in Architecture* (Cambridge: M.I.T. Press, 1965), pp. 20–21.

Schulz, a Norwegian architect and teacher, to make the single contemporary effort at composing a theory of architecture as a human product, in *Intentions In Architecture,* first published in 1963. Norberg-Schulz's integration of disparate ideas and statement of direction are warmly responded to by teachers and students.

Kevin Lynch's *The Image of the City,* published in 1960, is a tightly woven argument moving between concepts in perception and real-world research, resulting in an explanation of how different formal aspects of city design can be more and less legible to the person in the environment. Lynch's books and other writings have created a new vocabulary for urban design, influencing designers to use his distinctions and taxonomy as they conceive of new environments; and in this way his work counts heavily in current real-world research.[3]

Christopher Alexander's earlier work in problem-handling in his *Notes on the Synthesis of Form* is the dominant paradigm for constructing a logical means of working through complex design tasks, using as his worked example innumerable "needs" of the population of an Indian village. In his more recent work, Alexander defines a "pattern language" in which the particular configuration of design elements to meet a particular set of situational conditions is intended to be used for any other similar situation. The way in which research findings from the human sciences are integrated into the patterns—elements of a building or site—is another of Alexander's major methodological contributions.[4]

3 Kevin Lynch, *The Image of the City* (Cambridge: M.I.T. Press, 1960); idem, *Site Planning* (Cambridge: M.I.T. Press, 1961); idem, "The City as Environment," in *Cities: A 'Scientific American' Book* (London: Penguin, 1967), pp. 203–212; idem, "Quality in City Design," in *Who Designs America?,* Laurence B. Holland, editor (Garden City: Doubleday & Co., 1966), pp. 120–171; idem, "City Design and City Appearance," in *Principles and Practice of Urban Planning,* William I. Goodman, editor and Eric C. Freund, associate editor (Washington, D.C.: International City Manager's Association, 1968), pp. 249–276; idem, "The Possible City," in William R. Ewald, Jr., editor, *Environment and Policy: The Next Fifty Years* (Bloomington: Indiana University Press, 1968), pp. 137–157; Kevin Lynch and Stephen Carr, "Where Learning Happens," *Daedalus,* Vol. 97, No. 4, Proceedings of the American Academy of Arts and Sciences, Fall 1968, pp. 1277–1291.

4 Christopher Alexander, *Notes on the Synthesis of Form* (Cambridge: Harvard University Press, 1967); Christopher Alexander, Sara Ishikawa, Murray Silverstein, *A Pattern Language That Generates Multi-Service Centers* (Berkeley: Center for Environmental Structure, 1968); Christopher Alexander, Sara Ishikawa, Sanford Hirshen, Shlomo Angel, and Christie Coffin, *Houses Generated by Patterns* (Berkley: Center for Environmental Structure, 1969); Roger Montgomery, "Pattern Language," *Architectural Forum,* January/February 1970, pp. 53–58.

"Acquisition of a paradigm and of the more esoteric type of research it permits is a sign of maturity in the development of any given scientific field," according to Kuhn."[5] These writings now represent the outstanding candidates for a current paradigm in environmental design—as it is viewing itself relative to the people who will inhabit what it creates.

Though designers' explanations of the relationship between man and environment are likely to be presumptive, anecdotal, ideological, or self-referent, they do not necessarily exclude truth or evade reality. But now we need to find ways of turning them into hypotheses which can be tested by the paradigms of the natural sciences. If we frame our hypotheses carefully, we may even help the natural sciences to explain more than they have been able to.

In this chapter and the next another possible paradigm in environmental design is outlined, in many ways extending concepts of Norberg-Schulz, Lynch, and Alexander rather than replacing them. The "esoteric research" made possible by the theory should turn out to be little different from the agenda which the human sciences have already set themselves. The kinds of data the theory organizes should help us to discriminate between physical environmental influences on people and nonphysical influences, so that we can be surer of making decisions that have the anticipated outcome. Instead of discounting the meaning of the physical environment to human well-being because social and economic forces are so much more controlling, we should be better able to state its definitive, even if limited, import.

This approach to theory has more to do with the personal scale of environmental design—as the compass of human activities that people have in their own experience while they go about their daily round—as distinct from their daily round in its community and regional setting on the large scale, and from their daily round in its most discrete setting of tool handling and body temperature. At the larger scale the extension into urban and regional planning of theory in economics and political science, which has so concentrated on the systemic influences of urbanization, industrialization, and bureaucratization, is well established and maintaining momentum in research. The understandings in the biological and medical sciences of the workings of the human

5 Kuhn, *The Structure of Scientific Revolutions*, p. 11.

body have, at the smallest scale, been productive in establishing relationships between enviromental stimuli and human responses, and again, a research momentum exists. But for the sequences of behaviors people have in their everyday inhabiting of the environment—as they go to work, clean house, shop, take care of children, drive cars, study—the "theory" underlying these has been taken for granted as "the prose we have been speaking all our lives." Chapin has commented that the "daily activity systems of households are particularly complex to identify and organize in spatial patterns, and perhaps this accounts for the fact that planning agencies have tended to rely heavily on an intuitive view of family activity systems."[6] With Chapin,[7] Meier[8] and Godschalk[9] are among those few not so sure of what can be taken for granted, in their work on human time allocations and urban activity systems as a basis for making neighborhood and city plans. Leighton's work in trying to understand and define individual mental health in a community setting is an example of similar interest in the person moving within his daily round.[10] A growing interest in European sociology on people's activities in space and time has been observed, but more to the purpose of

6 F. Stuart Chapin, Jr., *Urban Land Use Planning* (Urbana: University of Illinois Press, 1965), Second edition, p. 229.

7 Chapin, Jr., *Urban Land Use Planning*, Chapter 6; "Patterns of Time and Space Use," with Thomas H. Logan, in *The Quality of the Urban Environment*, Harvey S. Perloff, editor (Baltimore: Johns Hopkins Press, 1969), pp. 305–332; with Richard K. Brail, "Human Activity Systems in the Metropolitan United States," *Environment and Behavior*, Vol. 1, No. 2, December 1969, pp. 107–130; "Activity Systems and Urban Structure: A Working Schema," *Journal of the American Institute of Planners*, Vol. 34, No. 1, January 1968, pp. 11–18; with Henry C. Hightower, *Household Activity Systems—A Pilot Investigation*, An Urban Studies Research Monograph, Center for Urban and Regional Studies, University of North Carolina, May 1966; with Henry C. Hightower, "Household Activity Patterns and Land Use," *Journal of the American Institute of Planners*, Vol. 31, No. 3, August 1965, pp. 222–231.

8 Richard L. Meier, *A Communications Theory of Urban Growth* (Cambridge: M.I.T. Press, 1962), especially pp. 48–54; and "Human Time Allocation: A Basis for Social Accounts," *Journal of the American Institute of Planners*, Vol. 25, No. 1, February 1959, pp. 27–33.

9 David R. Godschalk and William E. Mills, "A Collaborative Approach to Planning Through Urban Activities," *Journal of the American Institute of Planners*, Vol. 32, No. 2, March 1966, pp. 86–95.

10 Alexander H. Leighton, *My Name is Legion: Foundations for a Theory of Man in Relation to Culture, Volume I of The Stirling County Study of Psychiatric Disorder and Sociocultural Environment* (New York: Basic Books, 1959).

allocating labor supply to demand and of estimating television audiences than of adding to any theory of behavior in the environment.[11]

None of these approaches, however, deals with the behaviors that compose the gross activities of recreation, work, shopping, housework, child care. Within these fundamentals of man's relation to his environment are the seeds of the theory I want to explore. The lack of theory at this scale has led to the present situation in site planning, in mass housing design, in neighborhood planning as Lynch describes it. The goal of theory should be to free us from stereotypes in order to move closer to discovering new truths about ourselves in the environment.

Ways of shaping city form arise by custom or, more rarely, by creative innovation. These models include not only large-scale ideas (satellite towns, greenbelts, or radio-concentric street patterns), but also many smaller elements: superblocks, gridirons, or U-shaped bays of row houses. Once applied and shown to work reasonably well, and sometimes even if never successfully applied, they exert a compelling force on future plans, by virtue of their very simplicity and decisiveness in the face of uncertainty. Their power lies in their usefulness to the designer more than in their effectiveness in the real world. . . . We cannot do without these stereotypes. The process of city design would become impossibly tedious for lack of such crutches, and the power of a clear form to seize the imagination of a designer is not a negligible effect. It is the use of such models without reference to purpose that is defective, as well as the poverty of our stock and the tendency to apply it repetitively, as if unaware of the vast range of potential city form. . . .[12]

We are unaware of a "vast potential" because we lack the concepts and methods for identifying the human diversity now captive in the designer's kit of parts.

The Inception Process in Environmental Design

This letter to the editor of *The New York Times* illustrates the kind of disjunction we have all experienced. There is no doubt of the need for closing the gap between what we do to make and change the environment and what people need from their environment.

To the Editor: I should like to add a footnote to Ada Louise Huxtable's splendid July 22 news article on the Hudson County Courthouse.

Mrs. Huxtable criticizes the modern trend toward functional courthouses. As a practicing attorney, I should like to say that

[11] Alexander Szalai, "Trends in Comparative Time-Budget Research," *The American Behavioral Scientist*, May 1966, pp. 3–8.
[12] Lynch, "Quality in City Design," p. 123.

they are not even functional. The architects do not understand the numerous functions which trial counsel, court personnel and litigants must exercise in the conduct of a case.

Like so many legal problems, this one of law court functionalism might best be treated historically. In the original Roman basilicas, which were designed as courthouses, the architects gave as much space to corridors and public areas as they did to the portions where formal proceedings were held.

They did this understanding that conference between attorneys and groups of litigants permits the settlement of cases more often than actual hearings. This understanding of the function of public space was carried through courthouse buildings erected as recently as the 1930's. Now, however, architects view corridor space as merely areas through which one must be allowed to walk while covering the least possible distance between any two courtroom doors.

Thus, in addition to learning something of beauty and spirit, as Mrs. Huxtable urges, our architects should also learn a great deal more about the practice of law and the practical aspects of litigation.[13]

I have said that we do not yet know what the right things are to do in environmental design and that it is worth discovering if a theory can help us to find out. The search for it best begins in the conception of new environments, as designers engage in the process at their drawing boards. The process can include making use of the past history of people's contentment with their environment, of previous urban growth and decay, of standards for the strength and appropriateness of materials, of aesthetic criteria, of architectural history. The process makes use as well of the personal characteristics and attributes of the individual designer, such as his gifts and training in creating form, his ability to empathize with people outside of his immediate experience, and his prejudices, biases, and values. These components of the design process are well known.

But a cluster of equally essential components not so well known relates less to the conception of a new environment and more to its *inception*: the original impetus for a new environment—that is, why it is needed and what it is to do for the people who will inhabit it. The originator of the new environment is the "client," which can be a city government, a firm, a university, a hospital, or a family. The process that comprises inception is so much less well known because it is so much less well practiced as a separate and distinctive aspect.

The mediator between inception and conception is the *design*

[13] John J. Bracken, "Letter to the Editor," *The New York Times,* August 1, 1966, p. 26.

program for a building, site, or neighborhood which ideally sets forth in writing all of the original reasons for the new environment and the goals of the client to be satisfied. The design program will list the numbers and kinds of activities to be housed, the numbers of occupants expected over time, their functional relationships to one another, and the special limitations that may be imposed by the funds available or by the climate or the topography of the location. The desirable physical qualities of the new environment may also be stated in terms of performance standards to be met, such as the thermal comfort level, the numbers of cars to be parked, the capacity of the elevators, the minimum size of apartments, and so on. Finally, the design program may include objectives and priorities relating to the health, welfare, happiness, and efficiency of the new inhabitants.

Horowitz describes eleven "major classes of information that should be found in most well-organized and thoroughly detailed architect's program instruments": objectives of the master plan of the city or campus; special restrictions and limitations on design; characteristics of the site; site development requirements; functional requirements of the facility; characteristics of the occupants; special facility requirements; relative location and interrelationship of spaces; budget; flexibility for future growth and changes in function; and priority of need among the various requirements.[14] He has also evaluated the programs he sees in his work on science buildings: "often of poor quality or . . . absent all together." Specifically, he finds that programming deals inadequately with the characteristics of the occupants, the relative location and interrelationship of spaces, and the priority of need among the various requirements:

Information [on the characteristics of the occupants] is essential for sizing of rooms, corridors, exits, and for determining the quantities of services to be provided. Information on the age, sex and even cultural and educational background may often provide valuable guidance in the development of the design. Most programs tend to be grossly deficient in this information. . . .

Programs should clearly indicate which spaces need special consideration with respect to location and interrelationship. . . . Many programs provide no information about this important factor. . . . This absence of data . . . may contribute to a faulty conception and the selection of an incorrect structural module. . . .

The cost of providing all of the desired features in a new building may exceed the available funds; therefore, programs must

14 Harold Horowitz, "The Program's the Thing," *AIA Journal*, May 1967, pp. 94–100.

describe the relative importance of the elements of the building program in such a way that the architect can achieve a well-balanced solution. . . . Most building programs have not provided guidance on this problem.[15]

The designer is always seeking a verbal description that he can translate into three-dimensional form and for that reason programs tend to concentrate on detailed descriptions of room types —classroom, office, laboratory, kitchen—specifying dimensions, equipment, electric and gas services, and the numbers of each to be included. Square feet standards for each room type—used as a shorthand for what goes on in it—may be taken out of previous programs for similar buildings. *Architectural Graphic Standards* is an indispensable repository of prototypes for elements—the stairs, doorways, lavatories—the designer repeatedly handles.[16] The square feet standards specified in FHA regulations and zoning and building codes also come as positive data to the building and site designer, because the variables he manipulates above all others are *size* and *placement*.

The circulation system linking spaces and determining placement should be the logical outcome of the relationships among the activities people are carrying out. The movement system of a building or a neighborhood is a major, if not the major, determinant of its physical form: corridors and streets shape and direct the elements opening on to them. But as Horowitz points out, specific locational data are often missing, and to substitute for them, the usual practice is for the designer to walk through the paper plan as a phantom user, asserting his own understanding of how it should "work." More often than not, the logical "movement system" represents the hierarchy of bureaucratic or social organization instead of the activities people are actually carrying out.

In practice, the data for the design program are chosen and organized more often by the designer than by the client—who is most likely not even aware that the program by which the new environment will be conceived is under his control. Due partly to this ignorance, partly to the awe in which they have allowed themselves to be held, partly to the client's selection of a "famous name," and partly to the lack of anyone else to do it, architects

15 Ibid., pp. 95–97.
16 Charles G. Ramsey and Harold R. Sleeper, *Architectural Graphic Standards* (New York: John Wiley & Sons, 1956), Fifth edition. See also John Hancock Callender, editor, *Time-Saver Standards: A Handbook of Architectural Design* (New York: McGraw-Hill, 1966), Fourth edition.

and planners make the studies and write the program objectives, if any at all are included—for in reality, the design program rarely ends up being more than an inventory of square feet standards applied to the numbers of secretaries, bookkeepers, lab technicians, students, children. For designers who have come to specialize in hospitals, schools, libraries or other large-scale and often single-purpose buildings, programming is already commonly practiced largely as a standardized information-gathering procedure augmented by the architects' wide experience of similar situations. Programs written by educational institutions, mostly universities and medical centers, are likely to be exemplary in explicitness and detail, perhaps reflecting the tradition of faculty and staff involvement. Designers have excellent reasons for wanting a decent program statement: the design process rests uniquely upon this guidance, and the maintenance of a good client relationship over several years of developing a building or plan depends upon an explicit understanding of many details.

The evidence is that the design program is coming newly into professional awareness. A leading architect declares: "There is more to architecture than function and form and visual aesthetics. How much more must be defined knowingly in the program. This is our next breakthrough."[17] The number of specialists in programming (usually architects and interior designers) is burgeoning, helping clients to provide their designers with accurate data. These programmers by and large stay out of the ultimate conception stage unless their professional colleagues invite them in. A recent publication of the American Institute of Architects on programming techniques describes one firm's attitudes plainly, incidentally identifying the central professional-territory conflict: "they prefer to work with architects on a job and do not presume to usurp, not even in part, the central and irreplaceable role of the architect as creator."[18] But what is more important is the

[17] Herbert H. Swinburne, "Change is the Challenge," *AIA Journal*, May 1967, p. 85.
[18] Benjamin H. Evans and C. Herbert Wheeler, Jr., *Architectural Programming—Emerging Techniques 2* (Washington, D.C.: The American Institute of Architects, 1969), p. 17. A general orientation to programming methods, gleaned from systems analysis, industrial processes, "critical path method," and human factors engineering is presented in William Dudley Hunt, Jr., *Comprehensive Architectural Services: General Principles and Practice* (Washington: American Institute of Architects, 1965), especially Lawrence Wheeler and Ewing H. Miller, "Human Factors Analysis," pp. 194–200; Louis Demoll, "Operations Programming and Planning," pp. 201–209; Louis

growing recognition that "the instruction of the architect in the development of a design solution" requires the collection of data and the development of criteria for any new environment.

In the past, architects have almost always dealt with historical building types. They knew somewhat intuitively which physical environment would suffice to meet the already well established patterns of activity of society. A bank was a bank, and a school, a school. Everyone knew what would take place in these institutions. A thorough and lengthy analysis of the institutional operation was not necessary prior to design. As society and technology changed and became more complicated, architects and owners had to look for new ways to determine the basis for environmental design. . . .

Contemporary environment is so complicated, and becoming more so every day, that the intuitive processes are no longer adequate for programming. Today's programmers must be especially qualified to conduct analytical, objective, unbiased, logical, and creative studies of the user's needs.[19]

Two Proposals for Change. For every addition to or change in the environment a design program is prepared. I propose that programming for new environments become the institution around which the revolution in the process of environmental design takes shape. The situation is now fluid, and before it becomes crystallized, basic and urgent questions about its content and methods must be dealt with. I propose the redefinition of the design program in such a way as to create a conceptual scaffolding between environmental design and the human sciences: the design program should provide the environmental designer with a statement of the inhabitants' requirements, which his work is to satisfy, that has been developed out of research conducted with reference to contemporary theory in personality, culture, and social organization. A design program developed in this way will specify so many previously unacknowledged human requirements that the designer is challenged to develop responses going beyond those presently in the vocabulary of forms. The amplification of the imperatives for new environments must inevitably have great impact on the designer's conceptions.

The key to bringing to life the many designers' "guides and checklists" of what to "take into consideration"—and they run through the literature like ghosts of answers to vexing questions

Rossetti, "Building Programming," pp. 210–213. See also Jane E. Hough, *Architectural Program Guidelines* (Washington, D.C.: Architectural Consultation Section, Mental Health Facilities Branch, National Institute of Mental Health, 1967).

[19] Evans and Wheeler, *Architectural Programming*, pp. 9 and 11.

—is a design program that uncovers these requirements and the priorities and values attached to them, in anticipation of the constant trading off between costs and feasibility that ultimately engage designer and client. That is what is either missing altogether in programming or being done on a low order of personalization.

If the programmatic dimension of buildings were not so clearly indicative of the intentions and values of the culture in which they arise, archeology and architectural historiography could not operate as disciplines. Yet despite this fact about the nature of building, professional architects do not, it seems to me, make enough of it in their programming efforts. . . . The profession should put out more effort to convince the client and user that every building project demands a close scrutiny of values, goals, purposes and present mode of social organization according to which clients and user conduct their own affairs.[20]

Probably the most valued guides and checklists for housing have been those of the American Public Health Association, published more than twenty years ago.[21] Panels of the most experienced experts of their time—in city planning, architecture, housing economics, public health, sociology—put together their considered opinions in the form of dimensional and qualitative standards to be used in drawing up criteria for neighborhood density, housing layout, numbers and sizes of rooms. Along with publishing these guides for the creation of new residential environments, these same experts published "An Appraisal Method for Measuring the Quality of Housing," to be used in methodically gaining evidence of environmental deficiencies to help in public policy decisions on slum clearance and housing rehabilitation.[22] Together, these guides to what to do and what

20 Robert Gutman, "The Sociological Implications of Programming Practices," *Building Research*, Vol. 6, No. 2, April/June 1969, p. 26. This issue has a special section on "Building Design Programming," with several articles by practitioners extolling its value and giving details of techniques found useful.

21 *Planning the Neighborhood* (1948 and 1960); *Planning The Home for Occupancy* (1950); *Construction and Equipment of the Home* (1951), all published by the Public Administration Service, Chicago, for the Committee on the Hygiene of Housing of the American Public Health Association. See also Anatole A. Solow and Clifford C. Ham, *Residential Environmental Health: A New Look at the Document "Planning the Neighborhood"* (Pittsburgh: Graduate School of Public and International Affairs, April 25, 1967), p. II-9.

22 American Public Health Association, Committee on the Hygiene of Housing, *"An Appraisal Method for Measuring the Quality of Housing: A Yardstick for Health Officers, Housing Officials and Planners, Part I. Nature and Uses of the Method* (1945), Part II, *Appraisal of Dwelling Conditions*, Part III, *Appraisal of Neighborhood Environment* (1950) (Chicago: Public Administration Service).

to avoid might be said to represent a paradigm for American residential design—reflecting a humanism still attractive today, and much common sense advice on practical matters. (No comparable materials have been prepared for office and industrial environments.)

But if advice of that kind or even more hard-headed research findings is to be put to use, the designer must be working within a context of explicit values and priorities established by the ultimate users. That context is usually undefined, indistinct, and inoperable. For example, research into auditory threshold levels will yield standards for the level and constancy of noise, probably expressed as a range, for varying noise sources and conditions. The designer can aim to bring the variables he controls into a combination that creates the consequences the standard calls for. He will have to achieve certain proportions among the volume of the space, the location of doors and ventilation ducts, the properties of the materials used in wall coverings and furnishings. But meeting an acoustic standard is likely to be only one of many goals of the design, all simultaneous and each almost invariably compromised to some degree. Whether or not the designer makes choices with reference to the client's objectives will depend on whether those objectives have been made explicit in the first place. If he makes choices without such criteria, he will probably rely on his own experiences with a similar building or his research into the building type. If so, he has decided on a product basis and not on a client or user basis.

But for the prospective inhabitants to be included in the design process with their full measure of weight along with the designer's biases, with the cost limitations, with the political considerations, and with all those inevitable and inexorable other forces, it is essential to have displayed the shape of their values and priorities. Two studies each have shown that neither human factors data—eye and hand coordination, ability to judge distance, and so on—readily available in a handbook, nor human factors specialists on the scene were used by designers making control boards and seating arrangements in aircraft. Without knowing what is more and less important to the users, designers are incapable of seeing beyond the functioning of the equipment alone:

Designers appeared unable to handle human factors problems effectively. They showed little interest in or ability to apply human factors data to their design problems . . . . Although it is possible for the human factors specialist to translate their design requirements into the needed human factors data, it is very difficult for the designer himself to do the same. *This is because, while designers can state the requirements of their design problem, they have difficulty in determining the information parameters needed to resolve the problem. In other words, at least as far as human factors is concerned, they do not ask the correct questions of their problem. . . . where their analyses tended to be systematic these were couched in terms of largely mechanical functions. Human elements were almost completely ignored.* Their design analyses were usually conceptualized in terms of black box inputs and outputs, with little consideration given to intervening operator variables. This suggests that even where design analysis is sophisticated (in an equipment sense) it does not necessarily include an adequate consideration of human factors.[23] (Italics mine)

And although the "human factors" mentioned related mainly to questions of vision, hearing, lighting levels, body measurements, and weight-lifting capacity, the authors conclude that

The primary means of ensuring the inclusion of human factors in design is through the design specification, since the design specification is the one information source to which all design personnel respond . . . we suggest that statements citing . . . applicable sections of the human engineering standard be incorporated directly into the body of the specification. The operational conditions under which the equipment will be used should be specified.[24]

An amplified program should yield for the environmental designer a means of explaining the decisions he makes about size, placement, circulation, equipment, and so on with reference to the inhabitants' requirements he is attempting to satisfy. He will have a framework for design that acknowledges the realities lying outside of the personal, the anecdotal, and the self-referent. Ideally, the designer should himself educate his client to want a rich design program, but in any event, the designer should have no fear of it: it offers him a new freedom to be inventive in response because he can concentrate on the possibilities he is trained to conceive—to invent new truths in space.

Although the designer could be a valuable member of the interdisciplinary research effort to develop the program, the very plurality and mobility of society today make it imperative to rely on the special study of man in order to comprehend his variety and to substitute for personal experience: a simpler,

[23] David Meister and Dennis J. Sullivan, "A Further Study of the Use of Human Factors Information by Designers—Final Report" (Canoga Park, California: The Bunker-Ramo Corporation, March 16, 1967), performed for the Engineering Psychology Branch, Office of Naval Research, pp. 24–25.
[24] Ibid., p. 35.

earlier world might have yielded readily to empathy and intuition alone, but now the participation of the anthropologist,
political scientist, sociologist, psychologist are essential. But *how*
are they to participate? Even as I suggest how, I am not, however, identifying supposedly eternal truths only awaiting ex-
posure to their place in the sun, for I do not believe that they
exist. I am only entering a plea for acknowledgement of the
designers' limitations—as any one specialist would be limited in
trying to deal with no less than the full spectrum of all activities
of society needing to be housed. Drawing upon his considerable
experience as one of the few sociologists working with architects,
both during and after the design program phase, Gutman com-
plains that the sociologist is often limited to answering questions
the architect sees fit to pose out of "the confines of his established
frame of reference. It would be judicious . . . for the architect
to recognise that the sociologist's commitment to the canons of
his discipline are as firm and compelling as those of the architect
to his ethical code, and a new strategy must be developed to
persuade both parties in the relationship to overcome the constraints imposed by the principles which govern their professional and scholarly life."[25]

The "new strategy" I propose, then, is the redefinition of the
design program as the instrument of collaboration, to involve
the human sciences as they have not yet been involved in creating a more humane environment.

My second proposal for change is that federal programs affecting the built environment should begin to fund—as they do not
now fund—just this kind of human study for environmental
change. For housing, research toward the design program should
become an allowable building cost covered by federal mortgage
insurance programs—as it is not now. For federal programs for
community facilities, transit systems, roads, and so on, it may be
a matter of extending and funding the often rather ill-defined
"pre-planning" stages, adding these human studies to the panoply
of economic and technical feasibility studies already required.
If funds were made available for a process that necessarily
includes the participation of human scientists, a new influence

25 Robert Gutman, "The Questions Architects Ask," *Transactions of the
Bartlett Society*, Vol. 4, 1965–66, p. 69. In this paper—the most comprehensive
discussion of many issues in interdisciplinary collaboration yet written—
Gutman is suggesting some of the reasons that "may help to account for the
poor relationship, the battle of misunderstanding, which now seems to
prevail" (p. 75) between sociologists and architects.

would enter their career and reward structures, and we might eventually see students and their teachers viewing collaboration as desirable for their own disciplines' development. Only the strongest of measures will legitimize interdisciplinary collaboration and move it beyond its present catch-as-catch-can condition, and funding is always one beginning.

One parallel precedent exists for this proposal: The Department of Defense regulations governing contracts for the production of man-machine systems—the mechanical and electronic equipment found most often in space vehicles—requires, specifies, and pays for a "human factors" analysis and plan. That language translates readily into goals for our larger living environments:

Military systems, equipment and facilities shall be designed to provide work environments which foster effective procedures, work patterns, and personnel safety and which minimize discomfort, distraction, and any other factors which degrade human performance or increase error. . . .[26]

The principles and criteria of human engineering shall be applied during concept formulation, definition and acquisition of military systems, equipment and facilities to assure the effective integration of man into the design of the system. . . . The human engineering program plan . . . becomes the basis for contractual compliance.[27]

Here is one software spinoff ready to be put to use in domestic programs.

The Douglas Commission has also recognized the complete lack of federal financial help for the design program phase of environmental design. The Commission recommends a "Design Development Bank" to advance these funds "for specific projects in low- and moderate-income housing, neighborhood redevelopment, urban renewal" to develop "ideas prior to the execution

[26] Department of Defense, "Human Engineering Design Criteria for Military Systems, Equipment and Facilities," MIL-STD 1472, 9 February 1968, p. 9.
[27] Department of Defense, "Human Engineering Requirements for Military Systems, Equipment and Facilities," MIL-H-46855, 16 February 1968, p. 2. The regulations, by themselves, are only the first level for attacking inherent bias: "If, as a member of the predesign study team, he [the human engineer] has had an opportunity to assist in the preparation of these criteria, they may contain most of these requirements. These criteria are, however, usually equipment oriented. . . . Far too often, unfortunately, insufficient consideration has been given in the predesign period to human factors requirements. The reason for this is the strong equipment orientation possessed by most engineering management." David Meister and Gerald F. Rabideau, *Human Factors Evaluation in System Development* (New York: John Wiley & Sons, 1965), p. 95.

of a project . . . using local needs and community priorities as a basis for design."[28]

Until very recently, almost all apartments were designed by 'apartment house architects.' Their charges were low and often they were not paid until the job was under construction. . . . They put as much building on a lot as the law allowed. And they used identical plans wherever possible. Whole areas of cities are direct expressions of this system. No one bothered with new designs. Apartments were a commodity to be bought and sold. . . . The great bulk of apartment building in the United States is still handled in this way. The FHA was manned by those familiar with the system, and change has come slowly. . . . A major part of the problem is the complete lack of financing for design and development prior to construction. When working drawings are completed, the builder obtains a building permit, construction begins, and the first call on the mortgage can be made. Three-quarters of the architect's and engineer's work is completed. There is no financing for this major cash requirement. It is understandable that every developer seeks to minimize these costs. Yet, it is the first fourth of this three-fourths of the work, the design and development stage, that should be given the greatest amount of time and money. It is this stage that gets shortchanged, although it is precisely this part of the work that produces buildings worth building and cities worth living in.[29]

The discontent with what is called "citizen participation" rests with this failure to separate inception from conception: public participation has up to now been invited mainly at the point of choosing among alternative plans as preconceived by the planners; it is all too rarely considered as the means of delineating the requirements that any plan should take account of. The planners are deciding both the objectives of the new environment and the means for achieving them. And so the institutionalization of the inception phase would also revolutionize the way in which power is distributed within the design process. If new procedures are instituted for the separate and prior process of plan inception, then the definition of the values and goals a new environment should try to maximize rests in the hands of the people, and the technician's role is more likely to be one of creative participation and less manipulative control. Instead, all the process permits now in the public sector is the breast-beating of conscientious planners who see that they are imposing their

28 Report of the National Commission on Urban Problems to the Congress and to the President of the United States (Douglas Commission), *Building the American City* (Washington: GPO, 1968), p. 499.
29 Ibid., p. 497.

values and biases in defining the problems they are subsequently responsible for responding to. The whole of my proposal can do nothing to end the inevitable conflicts among interest groups within a city or a neighborhood. But it can perhaps begin discussions of substance to replace wranglings over procedures.

If the content of the design program is amplified in the ways to be suggested, or in other ways, then we will at the same time be creating new criteria for evaluating the built environment we have now; and thus we may learn unexpected lessons from the experiments surrounding us. For surely we have for a long time been living in the kinds of environments that we are now debating—city and village, single-family detached and row housing, working in different types of office buildings and factories. But with what ideas about man have we been looking at these experiences?

Human Studies in the Inception Process

The concepts needed to overcome stumbling-blocks to interdisciplinary collaboration should be so clear and compelling that each participant can hold them in his mind as good and sufficient reason for working across disciplines—as a sustained enterprise and not simply as a fashion or a fad. That conclusion has guided the formulation of this bridge between the human sciences and environmental design.

The schemata by which man organizes his present behavior and anticipates his future behavior in a new environment, as discernible in behavior streams and circuits—that is, in identifiable and comparable units of behavior—are the focus of human studies prior to the conception of new environments. What man does in his present environment and what he expects to do in a new environment are the questions addressed by the research. Human scientists will study the particular (or surrogate) population to make use of a new environment to learn about their present patterns of behavior, their behavioral expectations and disappointments, and the values they place on them. The scope of behavior addressed in the research is defined by reference to contemporary theories in human nature, personality, and social organization from psychology, sociology, anthropology. The physical design on paper can be arrived at and subsequently explained by the environmental designer according to its intentions for fulfilling the behavioral expectations that space and its arrangements have something to do with. The management program for the environment is defined simultaneously with the physical program—specifying the people to run the building or playground, the hours of opening and closing, the kinds of activities to go on in it. The means of an eventual evaluation of the new environment's achievements are defined at the outset. Post-construction evaluation through observations and interviews can measure the extent to which the behavioral expectations stated in the design program have been fulfilled. The human studies, for these purposes, accept the individual as the smallest unit, so that studies of individual sensory functions, for example, are not the behavioral focus. In this way, the approach is meant to be mainly anthropological. The research and sampling techniques are any of those now in good working order in the human sciences.

The anthropological approach I am proposing to the study of man in his environment is a redundancy not out of place given the need to redress a considerable imbalance. The justification for it rests largely on the present condition of theory and findings in psychology and sociology, when it comes to understanding the relationship of man and environment at that scale at which the original conception of a new environment is made. The statistical findings of psychological and sociological studies are not qualitatively interpretable for the purpose of three-dimensional design.[30] Qualitative descriptions of behavior and its meaning to people can more readily be sketched or diagrammed in terms of relative size, location, height, and qualities of privacy, light, ambiance, and so on. Sociological studies of organizations are more likely to be useful at the next largest scale of environmental design, as when several buildings are being positioned on a site or the floors of a skyscraper are being allocated to the departments of a corporation. Socioeconomic studies of buying habits are useful for discovering the proportion of population capable of supporting large amounts of commercial floor area in

[30] "Market research techniques would not lead to the kinds of answers needed . . . [it] is cramped by the fact that some of the knowledge most needed can't be gleaned from nose-counting and percentages." Report on a Round Table Conference, "Human Needs in Housing," sponsored by the Menninger Foundation, U.S. Savings and Loan League, Capitol Federal Savings and Loan Association, 1964, pp. 79 and 81. "But to measure 'need' . . . is an entirely different kind of market analysis, requiring new criteria and methods throughout." Catherine Bauer, "Social Questions in Housing and Community Planning," in William L. C. Wheaton, Grace Milgram, Margy Ellin Meyerson, editors, Urban Housing (New York: Free Press, 1966), p. 34.

a new town, for example, giving the designers a basis either for concentrating or dispersing the shopping areas. Psychological studies, at the other extreme of scale, have much to contribute at the "performance standards" level of detail—in measurements of the efficiency of work performed under various light conditions, for example. People also can find "correlations" between their environment and their performance: they can vary the wattage of light bulbs and close doors against noise or plug their ears. Experiments are designed into some environmental controls: the thermostat provides a variety of performance levels, changed by the person from day to day, season to season. These small-scale properties of human response to physical stimuli help us to find out "how much" is suitable, but they are of no help in finding out *what* is needed in the environment toward human purposes. If we were to make a list of elements in the environment said to relate to human purposes in a positive way and another list of human purposes the environment can be said to have something to do with, we would surely end up with a longer list of purposes than elements.

Behavioral Expectations. The concept of the "schemata," originating in the work of Head on nerve impulses and extended by Bartlett in his study of remembering, has led me to the concept of behavioral expectations.

"Schema" refers to an active organisation of past reactions, or of past experiences, which must always be supposed to be operating in any well-adapted organic response. That is, whenever there is any order or regularity of behaviour, a particular response is possible only because it is related to other similar responses which have been serially organized, yet which operate, not simply as individual members coming one after another, but as a unitary mass . . ."[31]

Various researchers have shown the schemata, usually in maps and drawings, proving them uncoverable and thus measurable and comparable.[32] The ways in which people have organized their behavior patterns in the past are likely to coincide with their expectations of their behavior in the future. People can be asked how they would want to change their behavior in the future, if at all, to discover what now hinders them from fulfilling their own behavioral expectations. But although we might

[31] Sir Frederic B. Bartlett, *Remembering: A Study in Experimental and Social Psychology* (Cambridge: Cambridge University Press, 1932), p. 201.
[32] For example, Lynch, *The Image of the City*, and Terence R. Lee, "Psychology and Living Space," *Transactions of the Bartlett Society*, Vol. 2, 1963–64 (Bartlett School of Architecture, University College, London), pp. 9–36.

presume constancy to the behaviors, there is no necessity for presuming that the kinds of spaces in which the behaviors take place have to stay the same. For this reason, the emphasis on behavioral expectations is intentionally a departure from "preferences," in that behavior that is satisfying is likely to be preferred, and people are more likely to have ideas about alternative ways of achieving satisfactory behavior whereas they may be lacking in preferences for what they have never experienced. By raising questions of detailed preferences for environmental ensembles instead of questions about the behaviors people find necessary for attaining their ends, the designer is hemmed in with limitations to his imaginative abilities, right from the start.

My hypothesis is that the person is aware of the outcome he expects from what he is doing and he will be satisfied with his behavior, and with himself, according to the level at which he achieves what he expected. His felt sense of competence is the measure. The corollary hypothesis is that people's own capabilities as mediated by the environment will determine what quality they perceive it to have—again, I suggest that they endow the physical environment with stimulus properties depending on the level of satisfaction they achieve in any behavior that makes use of it: their interpersonal behavior, their job performance, their everyday round, their quest for beauty. It is less the noxious conditions of environment that threaten us from the hand of the designer and more the absent opportunities and resources his work will offer up to the behavioral expectations people have.

In their book *Plans and the Structure of Behavior,* Miller, Galanter, and Pribram ask us to

Consider how an ordinary day is put together . . . . Whether it is crowded or empty, novel or routine, uniform or varied, your day has a structure of its own—it fits into the texture of your life. And as you think what your day will hold, you construct a plan to meet it. What you expect to happen foreshadows what you expect to do.

And to do what you expect, the authors say that you make plans: "You *imagine* what your day is going to be and you make *plans* to cope with it. Images and plans. What does modern psychology have to say about images and plans?"[33] I ask, what does the modern environment have to do with them? If the designer knows what people want to be able to *do*, leaving aside what they prefer, he can design things to help them. The best

33 George A. Miller, Eugene Galanter, and Karl H. Pribram, *Plans and the Structure of Behavior* (New York: Henry Holt, 1960), pp. 5 and 6.

way of expressing data for a designer of physical things is in terms of *enacted behavior* that uses space, place, frequency, duration, extent, objects, and other people to accomplish its purposes. Once described, it is possible to know which behavior needs or does not need physical support or acknowledgement in the environment.

The actual movement of the whole individual, carrying out his various purposes, is a primary component of a theory of human nature for environmental design. He moves by foot, by car, by bus, by plane. He sees many objects and people at varying rates of speed, at various levels of detail. His motor coordination is in play: lifting feet to climb up and down curbs, stairs, ramps; using arms to open doors; using eyes and ears together to locate himself in space, both for orientation and avoidance of physical danger; balancing on moving elements (buses, escalators, trains). But the "individual" is only a convenient model for analysis, because in actual fact, environmental design is necessarily concerned with many individuals carrying out similar and dissimilar purposes at the same time.

If we generalize "expectations" into "what people want"—which might rightly enough be said to be merely another way of stating them—then we run the risk that the designer is faced with the same old blunt drawing pencil unable to put words into forms. What people say they "want" are, more often than not, the utterly nonoperational, exhortatory goals that designers would like to fulfill, but how? People "want to be *comfortable,* to work *efficiently,* to feel *satisfaction,* to have a *big enough* office." The first reason for reducing "what people want" to the nonverbal, motor behaviors they expect to engage in is, then, part and parcel of the necessity to discuss people in terms having unique meaning for environmental design. Likewise, by not separately collecting quantitative data about attitudes, opinions, values, and preferences, but instead by seeing them embodied in what people do and expect to do, we are beginning to understand people in terms having much more direct meaning in three dimensions. We are in a better position to find out just how effective or competent people feel doing the things that matter to them. In all, the quest is not for a theory of human nature for political science, or epidemiology, or interpersonal relations —but for the designing of physical settings in which people are doing things for a variety of reasons.

And so we are able to perceive criticisms of environments as expressions of the level to which people's purposes have been hindered from fulfillment—that is, the person's expectations of the behaviors the environment would allow or enable him to engage in were not met at all or were not met adequately. Some level of frustration or stress is felt and some kind of adaptive behavior is used. Disappointment of behavioral expectations experienced at a very high level leads to the all too common characterization of environments as "inhuman."

The concept of human stress is the toll taken by internal conflicts and external threats in coping with the ordinary and extraordinary of life. It shows up in aging and various kinds of disequilibrium—biological damage, mental illness. Overcrowding is one kind of stressful situation shown in experiments with rats to "accentuate social withdrawal and the prevalance and severity of behavioral pathologies."[34] Perhaps it will be possible to show that human overcrowding leads to the disappointment of behavioral expectations, thwarted by too many people having the same expectations at the same time and too few environmental resources for fulfilling them. The disappointment leads to frustrations and adaptations. On the other side of the question, the concept helps to explain the absence of stress where objective conditions would seem to warrant it: I wonder if we might find in Singapore, Hong Kong, and Dutch cities, with densities among the highest in the world, subtle timing adjustments or cultural mores that restrict various kinds of behavioral expectations and fulfillments to relatively few people at any one time.[35] The ferment engendered by the "rising expectations" of deprived

34 John B. Calhoun, "Ecological Factors in the Development of Behavioral Anomalies," in *Comparative Psychopathology—Animal and Human*, J. Zubin and H. F. Hunt, editors (New York: Grune & Stratton, 1967), p. 50.

35 In a study of housing conditions and social disorganization, Loring found that his data necessitated the rejection of an association between physically poor housing and social disorganization, but he was able instead to formulate the hypothesis that the "social density, definable in terms of social or cultural roles simultaneously acting in given physical space" contributes to conflicts and stress. William C. Loring, Jr., "Housing Characteristics and Social Disorganization," *Social Problems*, Vol. 4, No. 3, January 1956, pp. 164–166. See also F. Stuart Chapin, "Social Effects of Good Housing: A Sociological Experiment," in *Housing for Health* (Lancaster, Pa.: Science Press Printing Co., 1941), pp. 140–158 for the introduction of "use-crowding" —where the living room is used also for eating, cooking, or sleeping—as a measure of housing conditions. A French study found a relationship between space per person in households and social pathology; see Paul Chombart de Lauwe, *Famille et Habitation I. Sciences Humaines et Conceptions de l'Habitation* (1959) and *II. Un Essai D'Observation Expérimentale* (1960) (Paris: Centre National de la Recherche Scientifique).

groups comes not from having expectations, rather from the stresses of finding them unrealized. The challenge of sending a man in a capsule to the moon consists, in these terms, of engineering within a single small space resources for the fulfillment of a wide range of behavioral expectations—or narrowing the man's usual range—in order to keep him feeling effective, competent, and sane.

Stress research is being used to document the environmental sources of disease and disability, but we lack a parallel concept to guide investigations proving what is health-producing. Knowing more about the consequences of stress-producing situations may help to avoid some things at the drawing board, but that is not the same as being able to design those things which are likely to work positively toward human fulfillment. The concept of behavioral expectations—and the degree to which they are, first of all, related to environmental resources and then, the degree to which resources meet them—may help to move us beyond environments that are merely residually protective or hygienic. Only after the minima are satisfied have we set the individual at the "threshold of his potentialities."

Society in its full sense . . . is never an entity separable from the individuals who compose it. No individual can arrive even at the threshold of his potentialities without a culture in which he participates. Conversely, no civilization has in it any element which in the last analysis is not the contribution of an individual. Where else could any trait come from except from the behaviour of a man or a woman or a child?[36]

What kinds of things do people have expectations about? The scope of human expectations is no less than that of human nature itself. When I say that the "scope of behavior addressed in the research is defined by reference to contemporary theories in human nature, personality, and social organization," I intend that human scientists will uncover the behavioral expectations arising out of a full palette of human experience. Chapter three looks at this question and its consequences for environmental design.

Units for Analysis: Behavior Circuits. The design program concentrates on what people do now and what they expect to do in a new environment. We need next to develop the means of learning the content of the behaviors and the relative values placed on them. And in order to do that, we need units of be-

36 Ruth Benedict, *Patterns of Culture* (Boston: Houghton Mifflin Co., 1934), p. 253.

havior that can be observed, recorded, and compared. What we should end up with is a unit of analysis that serves both the human scientists' interests in behavior, its context and structure, and the designers' need for data translatable to form.

In the traditional formulations of the social sciences, the *role* is considered to be the smallest unit in the social system, as one way of categorizing what a person does and placing him in a system of social and interpersonal interaction. The approach in sociology and political science is to join many kinds of roles into substructures of society by abstracting from persons—corporations, kinship groups, bureaucracies, unions, cities. As entities, these have been studied systematically. In urban planning, architecture, and engineering, a unique concept of the "smallest human unit" is not now agreed upon. And I think we cannot discount the habits of mind instilled by the concept of role. The role a person "plays" abstracts him from that which he is and does in concrete and specific terms. In all the behavioral detail that makes up a working day in a working environment, the "role of the executive" is different from "what an executive does." The concept of role has given the designer of physical things the idea that roles are people.

And so, in order to uncover the data that will help us, the first step is to divide behaviors by their scale and generality. The things that people do at the widest compass are *behavior streams* or *activities,* such as recreation or work. These in turn are separable into units which I call *behavior circuits,* differentiated by specific purpose—such as a game of catch or assembling microwave components. These in turn are composed of particular *actions*—running around the bases or wiring the antennas. These more discrete actions are sequenced to produce specific outcomes and are subject to short-term stimuli, in contrast to the streams and circuits which subsume and generalize them. Actions are customarily measurable in terms of their rate or level of performance. Activities may be named differently, but they may be composed of behavior circuits and actions that are demonstrably similar. Behavior circuits may be similar in the actions composing them but have different outcomes. By behavior circuit I mean to denote both the movement and the completion integral to tasks, errands, recreation, work, visiting, and so on. The study of the man-machine relationship, when fingers, eyes, and elbows function with small-scale equipment, is called ergonomics; what behavior circuits implies is an anthropological ergonomics, tracking people's behaviors through the fulfillment of their everyday purposes at the scale of the room, the house, the block, the neighborhood, the city in order to learn what resources—physical and human—are needed to support, facilitate, or enable them.

A change in emphasis from that of *being in* the environment to one of *doing things in it* is a step, then, that leads to uncovering the kind of data that will help in the creation of congruent environments. The work of Barker in ecological psychology, Harris in anthropology, and Aas in sociology, as they have developed criteria for defining behavior streams, episodes, scenes, and settings, has led me to develop the concept of behavior circuits in order to bring White's concept of the sense of competence into an understanding of environment as providing the resources for behaviors in which the person's felt sense of competence is a crucial aspect.[37] The behavior circuit is a unit of analysis that permits this combination of concepts to be operational, as the round of behaviors people engage in in order to accomplish each of their purposes, from start to finish. The physical and human resources needed for carrying out the full circuit of behavior in fulfillment of its purposes can be identified. The question for research becomes—as suggested earlier—people's own evaluation of their sense of competence and objective measures of it, relative to the availability, extent, quality, and placement of environmental resources, human and nonhuman. The malaise of alienation can be pinpointed beyond rhetoric about our "dehumanizing" environment, and our criticisms can be stated more importantly than the "inefficiency" and "inconvenience" of urban life.

Though we may start out naming and agreeing on ubiquitous behavior circuits—marketing, the daily walk to school, cooking Sunday dinner, playing football—there is every reason to think that in looking for them, the concept of behavior circuits will reveal realities previously unrecognized. The very process of

[37] Roger G. Barker, *Ecological Psychology: Concepts and Methods for Studying the Environment of Human Behavior* (Stanford: Stanford University Press, 1968); Roger G. Barker, editor, *The Stream of Behavior: Explorations of Its Structure and Content* (New York: Appleton-Century-Crofts, 1963); Marvin Harris, *The Nature of Cultural Things* (New York: Random House, 1964); Dagfinn Aas, "The Impact of the Environment—On Bringing the Environment Into The Analysis of Behavior," August 1967, Center for Research in Social Behavior, University of Missouri, mimeo, 54 pp.; Robert W. White, "Ego and Reality in Psychoanalytic Theory: A Proposal Regarding Independent Ego Energies," *Psychological Issues*, Volume III, No. 3, Monograph 11, 1963.

defining the behaviors composing a single circuit will reveal the subtleties of cultural diversity and cultural change. Strauss has seen as an "urgent task of urban theory" the development of categories and related hypotheses about "the differential symbolism of space, and the differential behavior associated with that symbolism," as in the territorial claims of various groups, by age and ethnicity. He also would like to see the mapping of the "more subtle meanings of space for the city's residents" but he finds that "data and concepts for making such maps do not exist."[38] Perhaps behavior circuits can help. They should provide exactly the kind of data found missing in this critique of a plan for a Model Cities area in Chicago, written by an architect and former resident:

While the study succeeds in providing a methodology to program recreational facilities for the body, the design research team apparently lacks a deep understanding of the life style and goals of this predominantly black community, and thus, for instance, fails to provide young people with leisure-time spaces to stimulate the development of their minds. . . .

The Negro has never been a client before and we know next to nothing about his attitudes on density patterns, FHA space standards and room arrangements for larger families, or about how he uses open spaces, and how he values time and property. . . .

The proposal for the Douglas Boulevard Spine is saturated with playgrounds and passive recreation areas. No provisions are made for creative recreation or for the leisure time needs of teen-age girls. The proposal completely ignores the need to provide cultural facilities which stimulate the development of the mind or to demonstrate to other residents of the community and city that black civilizations have achieved historical milestones worthy of admiration. . . .

Lawndale is desperately in need of day-care centers, which could be built on vacant lots so as to give working mothers a place to leave their children within walking distance of their homes. . . .

Very little documentation exists on the character of the black community as a basis for planning. Although numerous studies have explored the effects of crowding on white mice, nobody has carefully analyzed the attitudes of black men concerning open space—analyzing, for example, how the streets of the ghetto serve as living rooms of the community. . . . Design formulas

38 Anselm L. Strauss, "Urban Research Strategies," in *Urban Policy Research*, Schnore and Fagin, editors (Beverly Hills: Sage Publications, 1967), pp. 58–59. Strauss has used the term "orbits" to categorize the "spatial movements of members of social worlds"—behavior circuits can be thought of as aggregating into such "orbits." See Strauss, *Images of the American City* (New York: Free Press of Glencoe, 1961), p. 66.

created in graphics studios and computer centers will help little to stimulate social interaction, economic integration, and political progress unless one adds the ingredients of intuition and respect for the life style and requirements of people from different cultural backgrounds.[39]

If behavior circuits do provide data that physical designers learn to make use of, they undoubtedly will have to reformulate their categorizations of activities, spaces, and their separation and linkages. The data arising out of behavior circuit analysis are likely to be untidy—overlapping, conflicting, simultaneous. The struggle will be between the designer's preconceptions and what the data reveal: his job of creating order out of human values is a much deeper challenge than that of creating order out of physical disorder. When realms, zones, hierarchies, and all the other tools in his kit are themselves the organizing principles, instead of handmaidens to human purposes and priorities, we are merely back on the bus keeping to its time schedule by not stopping for passengers.

The argument is, after all, with the precedence of and domination by techniques and artifacts over human facts. And one vital human fact always a part of the design of any new environment is a natural conflict among objectives: large but cheap, high density but low to the ground, landscaped but easily maintained, parking for cars but an abundance of play space, private backyards but baseball fields, parking close to home but invisible, stores nearby but residential property values unthreatened, bus service but not inside a subdivision, playspace near home but not noisy, large room sizes but low-cost housing—and on and on. I am arguing for the reconciliation of such conflicts by suggesting a way of understanding just what composes them, and not for my capability to do so. Ideology has played such an important part in environmental design, in its various schools and coteries, in that the absence of data seems to be compensated for by the strength of the commitment to prototypical physical arrangements.

In the same way, working anthropologists in underdeveloped countries constantly face the problem of responding inductively: how to guide change without destroying cultural values, while at the same time introducing genuine improvements. To be avoided are what Foster calls "pseudoimprovements"—when they

[39] W. Joseph Black, "A Farsighted Study and Some Blind Spots," *Architectural Forum*, December 1968, pp. 44–49.

have been derived from professional formulae and when their social costs outweigh their advantages:

Planning and design for improvements in directed change programs are executed by members of the several professions: architects, engineers, city and regional planners, agricultural and irrigation specialists, public health physicians and nurses, educators, and many others. Almost always they define "problems" within their narrow professional frameworks, and they seek answers within the same context. . . . "Improved" design as seen by the professional is not necessarily improved design as seen by the potential user. The best solution to a specific need is not a professional absolute, capable of application anywhere in the world. . . . If "improved" designs or recommended practices do serious violence to any of the social, cultural, or psychological needs and expectations of the people involved, they probably will be rejected. These expectations and needs are not necessarily obvious, as countless failures in technical aid programs testify. Often they must be ferreted out by research and analysis. Then, when they are understood, the plan most likely to achieve project goals, and meet local needs, can be designed and executed.[40]

The concept of behavior circuits can reorganize the way we view reality, with two especially important consequences. The first is that we are prepared to be alert for differences and to design in terms of them. The world can be combed for live examples of different conditions, both in the physical prototypes (e.g. linear or grouped shopping centers) and in the kinds of population using them (e.g. professionals in high-rise apartments; middle-income, Midwestern suburbanites). The differences in behavior circuits can be uncovered both by observation (making movies) and by asking people what is a source of stress or strain in the carrying out of their daily rounds. The same behavior circuit might be scored differently for each of ten or twenty populations differing in age, residential location, educational attainment, ethnicity, income, car-ownership, and so on, casting the imperative for differing environmental resources, in kind, interval, density, and so on. Even if behavior circuits are not actually recorded in minute detail, the concept is the basis for "discrimination training." To illustrate, the concept of behavior circuits can be seen to handle each of these criticisms Katz recorded after examining more than seven hundred housing sites, large and small, big city and small town, with and without federal assistance:

[40] George M. Foster, *Applied Anthropology* (Boston: Little, Brown and Co., 1969), pp. 6–7.

The challenge of working out an individualized plan—one that fits the site, climate, and special human needs—is frequently ignored. Instead the designer falls back on a convenient stock of "samples" applicable to all site situations. . . . Some of the most glaring shortcomings of contemporary site planning practice include lack of privacy, failure to design for daily and seasonal variations, impermanence of site details, unimaginative landscape treatment, unusability of open space, and poor relationships of interior and exterior spaces. . . . There was little evidence of special provisions for shelter, security, and lighting to make the sites usable at all times. . . . To create vital, attractive spaces and to conserve land, a site should be laid out with specific activities in mind and not left to chance. Usability is a consequence of planning and not a label. . . . Having given priority to the auto-mobile, planners give little thought to the resident as a pedestrian. The route from the parking lot to the dwelling is seldom considered. Instead, buildings are oriented to the street as though the majority of pedestrians approached the site from a corner bus stop. The front door is the show place, but for most tenants the back door—undesigned and cluttered though it may be—is the real entrance. . . . Emphasis on housing sites continues to center on facades and interior arrangements and not on site development. Buildings are designed from the "outside-in" and not from the "inside-out". . . . Differences among families are not reflected in current site planning practice. Most designs cater only to a monolithic, middle-class society. More advanced analysis, programming, and testing of tenant desires prior to design would reveal that there is great variation in the needs of families, even those that outwardly appear to be similar. . . . After construction, there should be some evaluation of both site and building to ascertain if, and how well, a project meets occupant needs.[41]

A second consequence of thinking in terms of behavior circuits is that we may discover a new relationship between numbers of people and the amount of space needed to accommodate them —that is, new measures of population *density* become possible. The issue of overcrowding, both upon the land and in particular spaces, is constantly faced in environmental design. Because the *time dimension* of behavior circuits is integral to analysis, it is possible to plan for use of environments according to the span of use of a particular space.[42] Designers need to be able to fore-

41 Robert D. Katz, *Design of the Housing Site* (Urbana: University of Illinois, 1966).
42 "For a humble example of the economic effects of people spread through time of day, I will ask you to think back to a city sidewalk scene: the ballet of Hudson Street. The continuity of this movement (which gives the street its safety) depends on an economic foundation of basic mixed uses." Jane Jacobs, *The Death and Life of Great American Cities* (New York: Random House, 1961), p. 153.

see that one kind of space will be underused at some time of day or season and another overcrowded. The introduction of time to control the level of use becomes possible only when the patterns of use are known—as shifts in dining facilities, express elevator service at peak hours of use, the dual use of the same space by groups whose timing is different. One behavior circuit related intimately to time is that of *waiting,* and as population rises and various services fail to catch up, it is, I think, going to become a human activity requiring its own physical and programmatic resources. It is not that various ways of timing the uses of spaces have not been thought of, but only that the usual design programming studies do not evoke supporting data, and so the idea too rarely influences the ultimate physical form. The scheduling of space use by various populations would respond well to the techniques of systems analysis and operations research, and especially to graphic computer displays.

Environmental design, then, pollutes the human environment when it overlooks and fails to provide resources in acknowledgment of the behaviors people have. The child in a high-rise apartment building who is going outdoors to play is carrying out a behavior circuit that upon complete description is found to include the action of urinating while away from his home toilet; to carry out the full sequence of "going out to play" to his own satisfaction, the environment for play must include a public toilet because the child will be dissatisfied with his own behavior if he has an accident while hurrying home. The person arriving by car in a shopping center often has a long walk after parking; supports to his behavior as pedestrian—clear and safe paths, shade trees, drinking fountains—are nonexistent. Young wives living in a new suburban housing development outside London learned that their expectations of carrying on with their marketing and pushing strollers while pregnant were utterly disappointed by the slopes left so steep as to endanger their health.

As one circuit of the behavior stream Shopping, the Food Shopping circuit on the following page illustrates that from beginning to end, the "commercial facilities" are but one of several resources needed in order to carry it out effectively. A Food Shopping Behavior Circuit is likely to vary as other objective conditions and behavioral expectations vary, e.g.: family size, frequency of guests, working hours of those in family who are employed, food storage capacity of cupboards and refrigerator, season of the year, bad weather; and concomitant behavioral

Food Shopping Behavior Circuit of Woman in Urban High-Rise Apartment

---

makes up list

organizes shopping cart or bags

arranges child care or takes with

leaves and locks door of dwelling

rides downstairs in elevator, or walks

walks, or rides bus, or drives car to market

walks: crosses streets, steps up and down curbs

rides bus: waits for it

drives car: parks in lot, becomes pedestrian

traverses supermarket, fills cart, checks out

watches child

carries bundles out: drives car to loading area; or carries bundles to bus, holds bundles on lap, gets on and off up and down steps, holds bundles on lap; or carries bundles in arms; or uses cart while walking home

puts groceries down to get out door key

unlocks main entry, pushes or pulls door, negotiates bundles through door

rides up in elevator or walks up stairs

puts down bundles to unlock apartment door

looks after children's toileting and thirst

puts bundles in kitchen

empties bags into storage areas, washing fresh vegetables and wrapping meat

folds up or discards shopping bags

---

expectations during Food Shopping, such as getting out of the house, learning about new products, socializing with friends.

A studio class of mine was to write the program for and then redesign a typical floor of a high-rise public housing project in Chicago. Students used the concept of behavior circuits to organize their observations of the present residents, and in tracing out their food shopping behavior, they duly recorded both distance and time from several points to the nearest supermarket. But when tracing out the actual circuit, they found that many women paid a fifty-cent deposit on the supermarket's shopping cart, wheeled their groceries home (for some, a fifteen-minute walk), waited the usual five or ten minutes for the elevator (if it was working at all), emptied the cart, and retraced their steps to return it so they would get back their fifty cents—hardly a simple matter of "going to the store." The students interviewed social workers who have a long-standing familiarity with the people living in the public housing, trying to trace out the patterns of children's play in what is acknowledged to be a threatening and dangerous outdoor environment. At first, the students learned that most mothers were so fearful for their children's safety that they prohibited outdoor play after school. Then, when it came to tracing out the mother's behavior circuit of socializing, the social workers revealed that for many mothers their personal isolation and withdrawal were so severe that they kept their children with them for companionship. The students had to face questions about the use outdoor recreation space is likely to get vis-à-vis a living room of minimum size; the designers of social programs might learn another operational definition of alienation.

Some behavior streams and circuits are ritual—worshipping, marketing in the open air, displaying and viewing collections of art—and their environments are responsively similar the world over. Some behavior circuits are so universal as to have had their environments defined in terms of minimum physical requirements accepted in virtually every industrial society: storing and preparing food has resulted in basic kitchen facilities; maintaining personal hygiene has resulted in the basic bathroom. It is theoretically possible to evaluate as an *asset* each physical and nonphysical detail that can be thought of or demonstrated to facilitate, enable, or reinforce the person's carrying out of his behavior toward its original purpose; its absence would be a *deficit*. Alternative designs for the same population can be compared for the assets they incorporate and the deficits they have, and it can be decided explicitly which and how many deficits will be tolerated. Convenience and amenity, which have often enough been considered trivial and expendable, can now be quantified in terms of human consequences. Moreover, new and better definitions of amenity become possible. Goodman says it very well:

Let me make a remark about amenity as a technical criterion. It is discouraging to see the concern about beautifying a highway and banning billboards, and about the cosmetic appearance of the cars, when there is no regard for the ugliness of bumper-to-bumper traffic and the suffering of the drivers. Or the concern for preserving an historical landmark while the neighborhood is torn up and the city has no shape.[43]

Indeed, the tendency has often been to credit the physical environment with an importance that belongs to the human behaviors it should be supporting. In a study made for the federal Public Housing Administration, Elisabeth Coit has observed closely "the difficulties encountered" in various parts of the environment of high-rise public housing.[44] She accounts for the difficulties experienced by two groups: the maintenance men, janitors, and management on the one hand, and the residents on the other. In using the excerpts which follow, I am trying to illustrate another dimension to the problem, not in the author's original intention. When these observations are read as though behavioral expectations and the circuits following from them are being described (even when the subject is a physical element), in some cases we find expressed behavioral expectations and a deficit in the environment and in others we find destructive behavior. It seems worth asking whether the destructive behaviors are related to those other behaviors frustrated from fulfillment.

Difficulties encountered in:
The grounds
Lawns crossed by unplanned paths or caged in by high metal fencing
Traffic snarls at building entrances
Corner cutting at walk intersections

Parking lots
Annoyance from noise and fumes
Space appropriated by nontenants

Recreation areas
Play spaces unused by small children and their mothers
Lawn areas used for play and digging
Play equipment marked up

The elevator
Crowded elevators with exasperating waiting time

[43] Paul Goodman, "Can Technology Be Humane?", *The New York Review of Books*, November 20, 1969, p. 30.
[44] Elisabeth Coit, *Report on Family Living in High Apartment Buildings*, Public Housing Administration, Housing and Home Finance Agency, May 1965.

Galleries [Outdoor corridors]
Danger that objects fall from or are thrown from galleries; fear of some residents about high places
Marking on walls; children's toys left about; wheel toys left about; wheel toy and roller skating annoyance
Lack of privacy; possible pilfering through windows
Cold drafts in dwellings
Snow removal in northern cities

The laundry
Laundries without attendance subject to disorder
Money stolen from cashboxes

Comfort in the dwelling
Awareness of neighbors
Outside world irrupting into living room
No chance to withdraw temporarily from rest of family
Lack of separation of different home functions
Inadequate bath facilities for large families

Safety in the dwelling
Children and objects falling out of windows; windows difficult or frightening to clean
Kitchen ranges placed at the end of a row of fixtures where children can knock against pot handles
Gas ranges near blowing curtains or having storage cupboards over them.
Slippery bathroom floors; tubs lacking safety grip handles
Electric outlets near water supply

Orderliness in the dwelling
Condensation within the dwelling
Wall space interrupted by scattered columns, doors, windows
Storage spaces inadequate, particularly in the kitchen.

The poor, passive lawn, just lying there, being crossed! The sad, neglected play spaces, and the mean holes in the ground! The effrontery of people, packing themselves into elevators. Why do they let children have tricycles and roller skates, after all? What a lack of self-control, not being able to wait for a bathroom turn! And dirty windows—not to mention letting their children fall out. Although the concept of behavior circuits may seem a somewhat compulsive method for uncovering what it is people do and value, it will hopefully reduce the likelihood of a persistent confusion: the primacy of objects over people.

Most psychological and sociological research so far has sought specific relations between performance levels for single actions and the physical supports to those levels: the light intensity for reading, carpeting to reduce fatigue and noise in hospitals and schools, background music in stores and offices, color schemes conducive to wakefulness. Experimental conditions are a natural research form for such seemingly simple correlations, so that not only does a broad and increasing reference literature exist, but the tradition of support for this kind of research does as well.[45] Research on behavior streams and circuits has hardly even begun. Barker documents how little studied *adult* behavior streams have been in psychology:

Of 643 studies of preschool children . . . 16 per cent . . . were observational studies, while three of 430 studies of adolescents (0.7 per cent) used observational methods. The proportion surely declines among studies of adults. . . . Psychology is surely one of the few sciences that has little more knowledge than laymen about the occurrence in nature of many of its phenomena; of talk, of fear, of problem-solving efforts (and their successes and failures), of laughter, of frustration, of being disciplined, of anger, of achievement, of co-operation, of play. . . .

Some other behavior sciences and some of the arts have not found the behavior streams so formidable as psychology has found it. The empirical study of behavior units and their temporal arrangement is a central issue in history, in linguistics, in music, in the literary arts, and in the dance. . . . In the ordinary course of life, the beginning and the end of actions are of utmost importance, for awareness of the arrangement of a person's own and his associates' behavior streams is the basis of effective social behavior. . . . Laymen, linguists, musicologists, historians, poets, novelists, choreographers, judges, legislators, and those few psychologists who have studied it, find that the stream of behavior is not a formidable datum, that it occurs in bursts, pauses, and pieces of many sorts which can be described and evaluated for both scientific and practical purposes. . . .[46]

Barker has noticeably omitted including city planners, traffic

---

[45] For example, G. H. Mowbray and J. W. Gebhard, "Man's Senses as Information Channels," pp. 115–149 and N. H. Mackworth, "Researches on the Measurement of Human Performance," pp. 174–331 in *Human Factors in the Design and Use of Control Systems,* H. Wallace Sinaiko, editor (New York: Dover Publications, 1961); K. F. H. Murrell, *Human Performance in Industry* (New York: Reinhold Publishing Co., 1965); Alphonse Chapanis, *Man-Machine Engineering* (Belmont, California: Wadsworth Publishing Co., 1965); Albert Damon, Howard W. Stoudt, and Ross A. McFarland, *The Human Body in Equipment Design* (Cambridge: Harvard University Press, 1966).

[46] Barker, *The Stream of Behavior,* pp. 21–22.

engineers, architects, and landscape architects from his list of
people who have studied behavior streams.

Techniques needed for recording diverse behavior circuits may
be simple to devise. What should be sought is a behavioral substitute for the verbal "time-budgets" and "activities diary"
favored by researchers into the question of how people apportion their time, a different question from *what people do* at
various times and places according to their purposes. Halprin
proposes "movement notation" as a "new tool for choreo-
graphing in the city."[47] Although he illustrates it as a way of
ordering a sequence of pleasurable walking experiences without
regard to their purposes, it is just the type of recording instrument needed for behavior circuits because it embraces movement at the scale of the designer's work.

In order to design for movement, a whole new system of con-
ceptualizing must be undertaken. Our present systems of design
and planning are inevitably limited by our techniques of con-
ceptualizing and our methods of symbolizing ideas. We know
only how to delineate static objects, and so that is all we do. . . .
Since we have no technique for describing the activity that occurs within spaces or within buildings, we cannot adequately
plan for it, and the activity comes, in a sense, as a by-product
after the fact. It is true that any good designer or planner will
think, while he is designing, of the activity that eventually will
occur within his spaces. But he cannot design the movement,
for he has no tools to do so. Even highway engineers who deal
with movement have no method of describing it.

A new system should be able to focus primarily on movement,
and only secondarily on the environment. . . . We need a system
to program movement carefully and analyze it, a system which
will allow us to schedule it on a quantitative as well as qualitative basis. . . . urban design should have the choice of starting
from movement as the core—the essential element of the plan.
Only after programming the movement and graphically expressing it, should the environment—an envelope within which
movement takes place—be designed. The environment exists
for the purpose of movement.[48]

The "kinesics" of Birdwhistell is a notational system for recording all movements of parts of the body—eyebrows as well as
hands—and, followed strictly, covers perhaps more detail than
designers can use.[49] Harris organizes his discrete classification

47 Lawrence Halprin, *Cities* (New York: Reinhold Publishing Corp., 1963),
pp. 208, 211.
48 *Ibid.*, pp. 208–209.
49 Ray Birdwhistell, *Introduction to Kinesics* (Louisville: University of
Louisville, 1952).

system of human movement into "chains, nodes, nodal chains, scenes, and serials" with what he calls "stage coordinates"—actor, physical object, time, and place—which begin to suit the scale and concept of behavior circuits, but he uses verbal descriptions solely.[50] I also add purpose and the expected outcome of behavior as the actor states them, which for both Harris and Barker are learned only inductively.

Thiel has also created a "space score" which organizes the physical forms perceived as the person's rate and direction change.[51] Appleyard, Lynch, and Myer have built upon this technique, placing the elements seen along a highway into such a "score" as a way of developing techniques for communicating both orientation to place and the experience of the person and his surroundings in motion.[52] But as with Halprin's choreography, these approaches are meant to help decide the perceptually pleasing location of elements in a landscape. The most precisely articulated notation system for recording the gross motor movements used with objects is to be found in the work of Frank and Lillian Gilbreth, who helped to Taylorize American industrial practices with time-and-motion studies of various manufacturing processes (Figure 1).[53] They spelled their name backwards (more or less, but certainly unhappily) to arrive at *therbligs*, a term still given to the symbols they devised for seventeen fundamental body motions, used to interpret slow-motion films of the process being improved upon.

No parallel between behavior circuits and time-and-motion studies as techniques for optimizing "efficiency" is intended. Rather, the opposite: by opening ways of ending those machine-like conditions of work going on in factories, offices, and institutions, where people are in possession of "an unemployed self," in Gouldner's especially evocative phrase, when their work and the conditions of their doing it seem to them a waste and a continuous confrontation with threats to ordinary human dignity.[54] Systematic attention to what surrounds their specific tasks, for

50 Harris, *The Nature of Cultural Things,* Chapters 3, 4, and 5.
51 Philip Thiel, "A Sequence-Experience Notation for Architectural and Urban Spaces," *The Town Planning Review,* Vol. xxxii, No. 1, April 1961, pp. 33–52.
52 Donald Appleyard, Kevin Lynch, and John R. Myer, *The View From the Road* (Cambridge: M.I.T. Press, 1964), p. 21.
53 Ralph M. Barnes, *Motion and Time Study: Design and Measurement of Work* (New York: John Wiley & Sons, 1968), Sixth edition, p. 135.
54 Alvin W. Gouldner, "The Unemployed Self," in Ronald Fraser, editor, *Work 2: Twenty Personal Accounts* (London: Penguin Books, 1969), pp. 346–365.

example, may reduce the intensity of that confrontation with conditions that diminish their self-respect. What does the behavior circuit of the food-break ritual really encompass, for men, for women? What are the behaviors comprising arriving, leaving? What expectations about personal grooming and hygiene do people have away from home that are demonstrably different from home? What behavior circuits characterize the use of lunch time, such as playing games and shopping? What kinds of behaviors are seen as natural overlaps between work and nonwork and which of these might be installed, facilitated, or tolerated in the workplace?

Name of Symbol	Therblig Symbol		Explanation-suggested by	Color	Color Symbol	Dixon Pencil Number	Eagle Pencil Number
Search	Sh	⟋⟍	Eye turned as if searching	Black		331	747
Select	St	→	Reaching for object	Gray, light		399	734½
Grasp	G	∩	Hand open for grasping object	Lake red		369	744
Transport empty	TE	◡	Empty hand	Olive green		391	739½
Transport loaded	TL	◡	A hand with something in it	Green		375	738
Hold	H	⏛	Magnet holding iron bar	Gold ochre		388	736½
Release load	RL	⌒	Dropping content out of hand	Carmine red		370	745
Position	P	9	Object being placed by hand	Blue		376	741
Pre-position	PP	𝄃	A nine-pin which is set up in a bowling alley	Sky-blue		394	740½
Inspect	I	0	Magnifying lens	Burnt ochre	XXX XXX XXX XXX	398	745½
Assemble	A	#	Several things put together	Violet, heavy		377	742
Disassemble	DA	⧺	One part of an assembly removed	Violet, light		377	742
Use	U	∪	Word "Use"	Purple		396	742½
Unavoidable delay	UD	⌐o	Man bumping his nose, unintentionally	Yellow ochre	△△ △△ △△	373	736
Avoidable delay	AD	⌐o	Man lying down on job voluntarily	Lemon yellow		374	735
Plan	Pn	⌐	Man with his fingers at his brow thinking	Brown	◻◻◻ ◻◻◻ ◻◻◻	378	746
Rest for overcoming fatigue	R	Ɛ	Man seated as if resting	Orange	ooo ooo ooo	372	737

Figure 1. Standard symbols and colors for fundamental hand motions. Reprinted with permission from Ralph M. Barnes, *Motion and Time Study: Design and Measurement of Work* (New York: John Wiley & Sons, Inc., 1968), Sixth edition, page 136.

Two examples more nearly approaching the concept of be-havior circuits—the only ones I have been able to find in archi-tecture and planning—are in Paul Ritter's *Planning for Man and Motor*. He reproduces a group of children's play-movements, although not shown in relationship to any physical elements (Figure 2). But a brief analysis by Christopher Millard illustrates

Figure 2. Play movements drawn by Tony Gwilliam. Reprinted with per-mission from Paul Ritter, *Planning for Man and Motor* (New York: The Macmillan Company, 1964), page 38.

with both human figures and environmental elements a scoring similar to Halprin's (Figure 3).[55] We need to develop symbols for representing the circuits of populations varying by age, income, car ownership, ethnicity, dwelling type, season of year, time of day, urban, suburban, and so on. Analyzing movies of the same behavior circuits in different settings endowed with varying amounts and kinds of facilitating environmental elements would itself yield rich, new understandings of man-and-environment. The analysis on paper could become a new kind of interview questionnaire, through which a respondent could show how and when he carries out a behavior circuit differently.

A Typology of Behavior Circuits. The human studies made during programming will not only identify streams and circuits; they will also discover previously unacknowledged hierarchies, intensities, and relationships of behaviors. These will become the basis for creating the physical resources needed for carrying them out. What those resources are determine the size, shape, location, distribution, and connectivity of buildings and sites—the very questions of environmental design.

The methods designers now use to understand the potential relationship between behaviors and the environmental resources they need contrast with the one I am suggesting. One method is that of "user evaluation," where the lived-in environment, after a social survey or market research, becomes a case to be cited as precedent for new decisions about what to include and leave out. Another is the survey of similar building types, usually published in picture books or magazine articles; far less emphasis is given to the actual use and more to ingenious ways of handling recurrent problems of form and mechanics. (Few people appear in such photographs; and when they do, it is always summer.) Mumford's classic *New Yorker* pieces on "The Skyline" and Jacobs's *The Death and Life of Great American Cities* represent still another method for uncovering these relationships; we could do with much more of their kind of insightful and critical eyes on the peopled scene. Ada Louise Huxtable, George McCue, Wolf Von Eckardt are some of the architectural critics featured in daily newspapers who carry on in this style some of the time,

55 Paul Ritter, *Planning for Man and Motor* (New York: Macmillan Co., 1964) pp. 36 and 38.

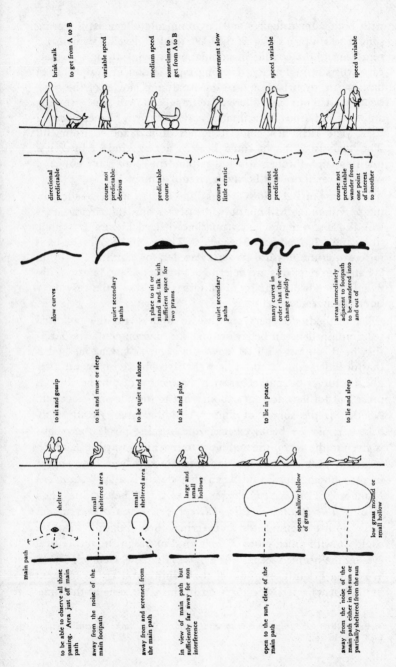

brisk walk

to get from A to B

variable speed

medium speed
sometimes to
get from A to B

movement slow

speed variable

speed variable

directional
predictable

course not
predictable
devious

predictable
course

course a
little erratic

course not
predictable

course not
predictable
wander from
one point
of interest
to another

slow curves

quiet secondary
paths

a place to sit or
stand and talk with
sufficient space for
two prams

quiet secondary
paths

many curves in
order that the views
change rapidly

areas immediately
adjacent to footpath
to be wandered into
and out of

to sit and gossip

to sit and muse or sleep

to be quiet and alone

to sit and play

to lie in peace

to lie and sleep

shelter

small
sheltered area

small
sheltered area

large and
small
hollows

open shallow hollow
of grass

low grass mound or
small hollow

main path

to be able to observe all those
passing. Area just off main
path

away from the noise of the
main footpath

away from and screened from
the main path

in view of main path but
sufficiently far away for non
interference

open to the sun, clear of the
main path

away from the noise of the
main path either in the sun or
partially sheltered from the sun

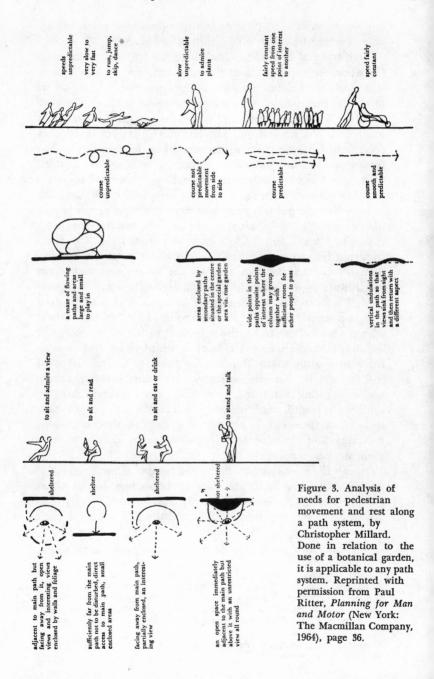

Figure 3. Analysis of needs for pedestrian movement and rest along a path system, by Christopher Millard. Done in relation to the use of a botanical garden, it is applicable to any path system. Reprinted with permission from Paul Ritter, *Planning for Man and Motor* (New York: The Macmillan Company, 1964), page 36.

but for the most part, their damnations (mostly of exteriors) appear after the buildings go up instead of before.[56]

Three types of approaches have been used to clarify the relations between occupants and their environment; although there is no reason to doubt individual findings, there is no way at present to extrapolate them beyond the cases they deal with, nor can these findings be compared with each other. Clare Cooper, a sociologist, has studied one public housing project thoroughly enough to come up with recommendations to designers of the future physical attributes similar occupants would be satisfied with. The range of both behavior and environmental resources she observes and discusses is encompassing and exemplary. She can specify from her interview findings what views people would like to see out of the kitchen window, the relative sizes they expect of kitchen and living room, the necessity they feel for a front porch in every dwelling.[57] Alexander's "pattern language" describes the specific requirements the future occupants have and illustrates in detail the physical resources devised to meet them.[58] Robert Woods Kennedy's *The House and the Art of Its Design* is written from the personal point of view of an architect who can well claim to be also a student of the anthropology of the upper middle class.[59] His book is meant to be used in dealing with wealthy clients building the house they themselves will live in, and he discusses entering, circulating, cooking, eating, bathing-washing-excreting, lovemaking, sleeping, housekeeping —all of the traditional functions of residential architecture. Kennedy treats them richly, however, drawing out their emotional meanings and demonstrating commonsensical details to help them work appropriately.

Though these writers (standing as examples of their respective genres) may sound as though they are prescribing for all places and all times, they would probably acknowledge readily that any designer reading them would naturally have to adapt their

56 *The New York Times, The St. Louis-Post Dispatch,* and *The Washington Post,* respectively.
57 Clare C. Cooper, "Some Implications of House and Site Plan Design at Easter Hill Village: A Case Study," Institute of Urban and Regional Development, Center for Planning and Development Research, University of California, Berkeley, pp. 275–291.
58 Alexander et al., *A Pattern Language,* especially the Appendix, pp. 59–283.
59 Robert Woods Kennedy, *The House and the Art of Its Design* (New York: Reinhold Publishing Co., 1953).

ideas to his particular population, climate, budget, available materials, topography, political situation and, not least, to his own imaginative capacities, experiences, biases, insights. And so, since that is indeed the only fate these guides, checklists, recommendations, and patterns can possibly have in the very real and various world, they accomplish nothing more than simply stating as fully as possible the particular circumstances surrounding a particular designing event. Trading cases among professionals of all kinds is an irreplaceable resource for education, for stimulation, for inspiration. An extensive series of notes on "what I think about as I draw plans" by a group of contemporary designers would be invaluable.

But we need concepts that unify the cases so they become comparable and can have valid significance for different situations. How can we find out when a Kennedy prescription should be followed, or a Cooper recommendation used? What reasons can we give to justify varying an Alexander pattern? A useful concept ought to yield the means of generating the varieties and combinations of environmental resources, either as the designer invents them or as he puts them together out of the store of prototypes. The concept should help to identify the conditions under which we do some things and not others. One such concept is the final component of my formulation. To recapitulate: the design program has been stated as providing the scaffolding to connect the human sciences with environmental design; the kinds and scope of human studies to be made for the design program have been suggested. The centrality of purposeful human behavior has been defined, and the behavior circuit as a unit of analysis introduced. Now, I suggest a way of classifying the kinds of behavior circuits there are in each behavior stream, as a way of helping to answer the "under what conditions" question.

The descriptive vocabulary in environmental design for classifying kinds of spaces and places is well developed: private, public, open, closed, dispersed; nodes, clusters, edges, districts, and so on. Analytical ways of stating what it is people do in the environment do not go much beyond sterile descriptions of "activities," but they turn out to match traditional land use categories, traditional building types, and names of room spaces. They are, in fact, mainly the *destinations* people have: school, office, medical buildings, community center, playground, playing field, residential area, industrial park, kitchen, living room, bedroom. Those categories should be only a shorthand for expressing the diversity of human behavior, but as they are used they are made to substitute for knowledge of what it is people do.

The types of behavior circuits I propose may not prove to cover reality adequately. They are meant to give us a rough means, first of all, for comparison. For any given group, we can find out which types of behavior circuits predominate and compare them with others. We can learn about cultural similarities and differences at a new level of concreteness. When we know the numbers of people in each type of behavior circuit at any one point in time or season of the year, then the density of one kind of behavior circuit can be compared with another, and new ways of measuring density and of timing the use of parts of the environment can be developed. Conflicts between behavior circuits will be more easily perceived. Newly emerging behavior circuits can be discovered, as manifest expressions of social change. We can become more parsimonious and pointed in research, because the typology helps us to see what we must gather data about.

Not included either as a type of behavior circuit nor within these definitions is *movement*, because a behavior circuit by definition *is* movement. The time it takes to carry out any kind of behavior circuit is included implicitly as a performance standard to be met by the design response. Movement from one place to another is readily defined in terms of time, and though it ought to be defined in terms of relative human energy expenditure as well, such measures lie in the future. If too much time or energy is taken up in one behavior circuit—that is, the completion of one purpose—then it lessens the amount available for another. Or people can be frustrated enough—by a long waiting time for buses, for example—to give up some purposes entirely. The psychological concept of positive behavioral reinforcement depends on the interval between the response to stimuli and the rewarding of it: the timing of environmental resources takes on more specific significance if the human consequences are measurable.

Behavior circuits are *routines* when they recur so often as to have a regularized sequence that the person carries out relatively unconsciously and more or less independently of others (personal grooming; walking the dog). Behavior circuits are *collaborations* when the actions composing them recur frequently but, unlike routines, go beyond the compass of the self to require other persons or equipment for carrying them out (vacuuming the house;

playing baseball). Behavior circuits are *events* when the maintenance of various kinds of group relations occur, at any level of frequency (parties, meetings, religious services). (A residual category is *emergencies*—for lack of a better word—which influence the shape of environment, as in putting out fires, where the turning radius of a cul-de-sac has to accommodate a fire engine, or in preventing fires, where the safety requirements influence the form of a structure.)

Each behavior stream is composed of behavior circuits of each kind. Cooking can be a routine, a collaboration, or an event. In each manifestation, it needs different environmental resources: cooking three meals a day for the family is a routine; cooking eight pounds of fudge for the charity sale is a collaboration; and cooking for a dinner party of sixteen twice a year is an event. What is a routine for one subculture may be an event for another—where having ten people to sit down together at a table most weekdays is routine for families still in an extended kinship system, it is an event where the nuclear family system predominates. Recreation for the same person can be a routine, as in the morning jog; a collaboration, as in the weekly game of touch football; and an event, as in attending the World Series. Recreation for different age groups may show chiefly one kind of behavior circuit: morning jogging is routine for those over thirty-five; playing touch football is routine for fifteen-year-old boys; and attending night games an event for elderly men.

For each type of behavior circuit, the most general kinds of environmental resources that are needed for carrying them out can be suggested as examples. Routines are ordinarily facilitated by drawers, shelves, lights, knobs, small hand equipment, doors, carts, paths. Collaborations may rely on mechanical equipment, desks, large containers, storage areas, other people. Events are likely to use whole buildings, and many repetitive elements, such as chairs and parking spaces, and larger numbers of other people. And each type of behavior circuit begins to imply its own performance standards or criteria for design:

For routine behavior circuits that relatively large numbers of people, or the same people, carry out repetitively, frequently, and at the same time, then the environmental resources will need, for example, to be plentiful, in the appropriate sequence, durable, pleasant, and require little adaptive behavior. Those environments charging a high adaptive cost can be studied to find out what *new* routine behavior circuits they give rise to, as when people climb stairs regularly because the elevator breaks down. On the whole, routine behavior circuits should have the physical resources of such a standard that the fulfillment of purposes is not constantly called into question. Subways and transit systems used constantly and repetitively by the same group of people could stand evaluation in these terms. The kitchens of public housing, as the actual setting for diverse routine behavior circuits (chatting, shoe polishing, ironing) could be studied for the extent of adaptive behavior their small size or sparse storage space necessitates.

For behavior circuits that are collaborations—where the individual's purposes are accomplished in concert with others and with equipment—the environmental resources will need, for example, to accommodate their numbers, the bulkiness of the equipment, and to be arranged (or arrangeable) in a logical sequence. Hospital planning is a model of the process of defining the physical response to collaborative behavior circuits: the routes taken to fulfill each specialized function are separated or overlapped, the equipment needs are made explicit, and the numbers of people in each behavior circuit at any one time are counted.[60] All too often offices are laid out according to organizational hierarchy when they might better be reflecting the movements of each collaborative behavior circuit.

For behavior circuits that are classified as events, the environmental resources have to accommodate a peak number of people, maintain physiological functioning outside of individual control at comfort levels (lighting, ventilation), and give clear information about the spatial organization to infrequent participants.

With this classification, the sources of environmental deficiencies become apparent in new terms. To generalize, for example, it is likely that routine behavior circuits are not supplied with sufficient environmental resources in and around housing sites and their neighborhoods within a few blocks (note the paths people make over grass versus the ones designed in asphalt). The density of people carrying out similar behavior circuits at the same time is insufficiently calculated (elevator waiting time; crowded playgrounds). Behavior circuits classified as collaborations are more likely to show a lack of resources inside buildings

[60] J. J. Souder, W. E. Clark, J. I. Elkind, M. B. Brown, *Planning for Hospitals: A Systems Approach Using Computer-Aided Techniques* (Chicago: American Hospital Association, 1964).

or a lack of places themselves (for the poor, the lack of resources may be in furniture and electrical equipment; for teenagers, a place for informal get-togethers outside of home). Behavior circuits that are events are likely to be *overly* endowed with environmental resources (the unused churches and schools open only part of each day, week, and season).

Behavior Circuits and Urban Activity Systems. Chapin has shown the most consistent interest in urban and regional planning in research into actual behavior as a basis for large-scale land use and circulation proposals.[61] The concept of behavior circuits fits well with his objectives, and because our approaches are so complementary, the differences are also revealing.

His work on urban activity systems has been undertaken to describe, explain, and predict "the way people spend their time and move about the city; to learn about people's differences in preference for housing; and to uncover their levels of satisfaction with the location and liveability of their environment."[62] Using these same variables, Chapin hopes to understand as well the people who move to a new housing location. His schema relies on understanding human nature as expressed, first of all in the need for "interaction" and "for security, achievement, and status, but also a residual set of felt needs, such as the sheer enjoyment of an activity for its own sake."[63] These motivations, in turn, are placed into the context of "human activity in a generic sense as the composite output of choices men make. . . . In making choices on how he spends his time, man consciously or subconsciously searches for an optimal combination of satisfactions based on the suboptimizations of security, achievement, status, and other needs essential to his sense of well-being. His trade-offs at a particular time in each suboptimal combination of choices are determined by levels of satisfaction-dissatisfaction anticipated . . . within constraints of income, stage in life cycle, and knowledge of the options open to him."[64] Chapin is interested in these occurrences at every time scale—day, week, year, life cycle—and at every spatial scale, including the regional.

The problem he has undertaken to explore seems to be that of apportioning: the distribution in space and frequency of use of environmental resources in rough accordance with the way the

61 See note 7, this chapter.
62 Chapin, Jr., "Activity Systems and Urban Structure," p. 17.
63 Ibid., p. 13.
64 Ibid., p. 15.

population apportions its time and activity choices, including the less frequently made choice to change residential location. The close study of household time-budgets, survey research to disclose preferences, especially for using leisure, and the use of gaming situations to explore the choice and tradeoff mechanisms are tools Chapin has called upon in putting his schema to test.

We are each dealing with a separate aspect of a similar problem—mine being how to learn what resources people need in the physical environment in order to go about their daily round with least adaptive cost and without diminution (and perhaps with increase) of their felt sense of competence; and Chapin's being to learn how to apportion the resources in the physical environment. The kinds of resources are taken as givens, just as people's behaviors are taken as givens. He tends to see dissatisfaction expressing itself in active choices people make, for which marketplace evidence can be found; I see it expressed in observable, adaptive behaviors, some of which might be enriching, some costly in well-being. Beyond changing their residential location, Chapin does not say what mechanism mediates between people's low level of satisfaction with the environment and aspects of human nature other than "deviant behaviors" and "nonconforming behaviors."[65] But in my terms, when people are "dissatisfied" and do not move, they adapt. This variety and range of behaviors is to be acknowledged by behavior circuits, not placed beyond the pale of normality. The middle ground of adaptive behavior is also singular evidence of social and cultural change at the microscale. In all, we would be clothing the facile term "life style" with specific evidence now lacking.

In Chapin's terms, what I hope to learn from research into behavior circuits would fit under "neighborhood and housing amenities (attractiveness and functional suitability to household needs and wants)."[66] He sees amenities as attractions which encourage people to move as a positive choice, not necessarily made on the basis of dissatisfaction. Again, our contexts are complementary but different. We share in questioning the economic determinism in which urban and regional planning finds itself enmeshed in explaining circulation and land use patterns of the past and projecting those of the future.[67] But because his

[65] Ibid., p. 15.
[66] Ibid., p. 16.
[67] Chapin, Jr. and Logan, "Patterns of Time and Space Use," pp. 310–11.

schema relies on an interlocking hierarchy of scales extrapolated from house to region, those more discrete data on behaviors people actually have are quickly converted into activity categories paralleling land use categories. This inventory is analyzed with the usual demographic and socioeconomic variables because those are the only ones available above the scale of tailor-made survey research. Partly because he is trying to explain such larger-scale processes, and specifically the location and distribution of land uses, community facilities, and circulation at a regional scale, there is the pressure to serve up data in digestible terms to the mathematical model-makers of regional growth. But this approach fails to allow a sufficient analysis of those very microscale behaviors that should be the basis for the kinds of resources planned for.

In recent work, Chapin and Brail report some useful statistical analyses to uncover the variables relating to how people use their free time. One variable of especial interest to the concept of behavior circuits is called "family responsibility," an "index inversely related to the age of the youngest child in the household."[68] It implies, for their purposes, the amount of time obligatorily spent in and around the house; they find that about 80 percent of people's weekday time in metropolitan areas is spent in and around home, and those with young children spend up to 85 percent.[69] How do room sizes, site layouts, play spaces, stores and so on enable or hinder people in their daily round where so much of their living is carried on? What adaptations have they made? How do their cultural and other differences express themselves in cooking, shopping, visiting patterns? What is the rate of change of these patterns? Although the authors' analyses offer the likelihood that it will be possible to use certain predictors to apportion community facilities and population on the regional scale, it is only at the microscale that we can learn more about diversity—what the authors themselves call "the nuances of human activity systems."[70] It is on those very nuances that planning for diversity and for choice depends, if only we will allow it to. We should be refining predictors at the microlevel—qualitative community studies are one kind, behavior circuits are another. In a study of the social interaction

[68] Chapin, Jr. and Brail, "Human Activity Systems in the Metropolitan United States," p. 121.
[69] Ibid., p. 127.
[70] Ibid., p. 128.

between public housing residents and the neighborhoods around them, Kriesberg has found that variables other than socioeconomic have considerable explanatory strength:

On the basis of the evidence from this analysis . . . it seems that the heterogeneity within a project and within the area surrounding a project is often large enough to provide the basis for establishing neighborly relations and even friendships. After all, people are not alike only because they have similar incomes or levels of education. They are also alike and share interests because they have other qualities as men, women, mothers, fathers, shoppers, wives, husbands, renters, residents in a general area of a city, and consumers of popular culture. . . . The evidence of this analysis indicates that socioeconomic status differences are not a particularly important barrier to social interaction between project tenants and neighborhood residents.[71]

I doubt that my approach to theory can ever explain large-scale "urban systems"; I know that no large-scale systems theory has yet explained what lies close to hand as people experience "amenity and livability." My approach to theory, such as it is, is intended to help us find out whether we are trying to explain those things that matter and whether we have already defined enough of what needs to be explained about people within their physical environments.

The Work of Roger Barker. Barker uses the physical attributes of the environment as he finds them; the question I am examining is how to create those attributes *de novo*, perhaps even in order to transform the objective reality we have called a "park" or an "office" or a "living room." I find uniquely in Barker's work a genuinely scientific source of such possible transformations. It seems unlikely that it is any longer possible to understand in full measure "land use planning" or "buildings" or "rooms" without Roger Barker's *Ecological Psychology: Concepts and Methods for Studying the Environment of Human Behavior* in hand.

Barker has sought to discover behavior in its natural form, "unaltered by the techniques of search and discovery," just as the elements have been discovered and identified.

We read, for example, that potassium . . . ranks seventh in the order of abundance of elements . . . that its compounds are widely distributed in the primary rocks, the oceans, the soil, plants, and animals. . . . The fact that there is no equivalent information in the literature of scientific psychology (about play-

[71] Louis Kriesberg, "Neighborhood Setting and the Isolation of Public Housing Tenants," *Journal of the American Institute of Planners*, Vol. 34, No. 1, January 1968, p. 49.

ing, about laughing, about talking, about being valued and de-
valued, about conflict, about failure) confronts psychologists
with a monumental incompleted task. This is the task of ecological psychology. . . .[72]

Although we have daily records of the oxygen content of river
water, of the ground temperatures of cornfields, of the activity of
volcanoes, of the behavior of nesting robins . . . there have been
few scientific records of how human mothers care for their young,
how teachers behave in the classroom, what families actually do
and say during mealtime. . . . Because we have lacked such
records, we have been able only to speculate about many important questions, such as these: What changes have occurred
over the generations in the participation of children in community life? How does life differ for members of large and small
families? How frequently is success achieved in everyday life,
and what are its consequences for subsequent behavior? How
does the environment differ for rural, town, and urban residents? . . . Before we can answer these kinds of questions, we
must know more than the laws of behavior. We must know how
the relevant conditions are distributed among men.[73]

Barker and his associates have asked and answered, "when an
investigator does not impose *his* units on the stream of behavior,
what are *its* units?"[74] They first discovered behavior episodes
and then found behavior settings. Both the theory and the
method for uncovering and categorizing behavior settings have
been achieved, and at the scale of an entire (real) town, Barker
has demonstrated an exciting, though perhaps unintended, redefinition of "land use." When looking for behavior streams in
their public environmental settings, the traditional classifica-
tions of land use and activities, as the physical planner relies on
them, have to be abandoned. The sheer number of environmental resources in these terms expands enormously because the
resources include not only the particular building, but places
and events as well—such as hallways, bus stops, scout meetings,
street fairs, newspaper reporter beats. Behavior settings are wider
than bounded space: a sidewalk is a behavior setting; a room is
not one until it is inhabited by people exhibiting behavior.

These data show that there are 198 genotypes among Midwest's 884 behavior settings, i.e. 198 standing patterns of behavior and milieu with noninterchangeable programs. If the
town were abandoned by its present inhabitants and resettled by
people of totally alien culture, they would require 198 instruc-

[72] Barker, *Ecological Psychology*, p. 145.
[73] Ibid., pp. 2 and 3.
[74] Ibid., p. 146.

tion books and/or training programs to constitute the behavior environment of Midwest.[75]

The behavioral meaning (output, he calls it) of these resources is also measurable—on the basis of the number of them in the town, the frequency or schedule of their occurrence, and their duration in time. He derives an "Ecological Resource Index" which allows comparing them with each other and with the same data for other towns. He is able, for example, to discriminate behavior settings in which the attendance of children and adolescents is encouraged and discouraged and to compare towns on the basis of their receptivity to youngsters' behaviors.[76]

In another type of analysis, Barker derives a measure of "occupancy time" for each of the "standing patterns of action" so they can be compared for the behavior they generate relative to their resources. For example, "more of the limited time of Midwest residents is allocated to behavior setting programs where Education is prominent than to settings where Recreation is prominent, more to primary Business settings than to primary Government settings" and so on.[77] The occupancy time, in turn, can be compared with the Ecological Resource Index to generate a new way of measuring "over- and underuse," as it is known: "The least productive action pattern relative to its resources is Religion; behavior settings where Religion is prominent generate 32 per cent of the occupancy expected on the basis of its resources . . ."[78]

Barker defines five behavior mechanisms every behavior setting has in some proportion or other: affective behavior (overt emotional behavior of any kind), talking (all forms of verbalizing), thinking (problem-solving and decisionmaking), gross motor activity (involvement of the large muscles, limbs), and manipulation (involvement of the hands).[79] His data show that the "greatest proportion of the time of Midwest residents is allotted to behavior settings where Manipulation is prominent and the

[75] Ibid., p. 116.
[76] Ibid., p. 124.
[77] Ibid., p. 130.
[78] Ibid., pp. 131–132.
[79] Ibid., pp. 68–69. In a review of *Ecological Psychology*, Karl E. Weick observes that "in 1955 there was far more concern with social behavior; 28 per cent of [Barker's] earlier book was devoted to social behavior, whereas now it is merely one of 11 action patterns." In Chapter 1 I have suggested that measures of the sense of competence are to be found and valued in behavior other than interpersonal and social. *Science*, 14 November 1969, pp. 856–858.

least to settings where Affective Behavior is prominent. Settings where Thinking is essential generate almost the same amount of behavior as those where a strong back (Gross Motor Activity) is essential."[80] He has also derived a General Richness Index, measuring the variety of behavior within a given behavior setting.[81] These are merely illustrations of the total approach to behavior as it exists for an ecological psychologist.

In environmental design, Barker's work is significant for the fuller range of behavior settings he enables us to identify, measure, and compare. He demonstrates that if we expand our view of what we see as behavior-and-environment, we can learn to see as well many more physical and human resources for carrying out hitherto unrecognized behaviors. Because of the way he constructs his theory of behavior settings, other people in them are an essential component. He is able, therefore, to discuss the designer's constant dilemma of "how big" any given behavior setting should be in a theoretical framework offering some possibility of prediction.[82]

In expanding the definition of environment to include time, people, exhibited behaviors, kinds of behaviors, and so on, the human and nonhuman resources needed can be seen more clearly. And looking for behavior settings means finding more behavior circuits: "Within a behavior setting there are routes to goals that are satisfying to the inhabitants. A setting exists only so long as it provides its inhabitants with traversable routes to the goals their own unique natures require."[83] A design program whose research has been guided by Barker's concepts is a natural collaborative experiment needing to be made, as is an "ecological resource map" of human activity to complement the traditional "land use map" of real estate activity.

The Urgent Need for Collaboration Toward Theory

At a time when we are in the midst of training so many environmental designers and creating so many new environments, some stronger conceptual links between the human sciences and environmental design have become urgently needed.

Architecture, planning, and engineering provide few criteria to bridge the designed environment with its satisfying use—perhaps only "efficiency," "safety," "economy" and, less often than we like,

80 Ibid., p. 133.
81 Ibid., p. 70.
82 Ibid., Chapter 7.
83 Ibid., p. 167.

"beauty." The vocabulary is almost exclusively in terms of formal properties, omitting any with which we might evaluate the myriad of consequences people experience.[84] By separating out the design program as anterior to the designer's conception of a new environment instead of being integral to it, the original control of these criteria belongs to the inhabitants, just as the environment belongs to them ever after. Unfortunately a prevalent attitude among working designers is, however, that their function is to tell the client what he wants. In terms of form, certainly that is so, but it is contemptuous in terms of consequences. Contempt—often used to cloak the frustration of not knowing—might disappear with more adequate theory about man in environment that gives rise to techniques both for making consequences more explicit and for expanding the kinds of consequences capable of being anticipated. One architect and teacher expresses the frustration clearly:

Our great problem is that we can't test what life and the environment ought to be, because there are so many variables . . . I don't yet know enough about simulation techniques of the computer to be convinced that they really work; I still have a suspicion that we will need to watch the organism in process in a number of alternative full-scale situations. . . . there are a large number of existing natural models that we could watch, but nobody is watching at all. If you go about . . . attempting to develop criteria for the design of housing right now, you find that there is little information that can be gained from any source. Nobody has watched and reported the existing conditions. . . . Little work has been done at the microsociological scale, without which we are hamstrung.[85]

A second source of urgency is the realization that the human sciences will have to develop their own hypotheses about the

[84] "Thus, whatever formal characteristics a work of architecture may share with other categories of art, there remains this fundamental difference: *architecture has no spectators, only participants.* (The weakness of most architectural criticism is precisely that it is based upon pictorial *representations* of the building, not upon experiential immersion in the building itself. This isolation of the visual dimension from the multiform matrix of reality deforms our critical literature and seriously reduces its value.) This distinction, so obvious and yet so profound, is too often ignored by everyone, including the architects themselves. All too often, as a result, any contradictions between the formal requirements of the container and the functional requirements of the contained is arbitrarily resolved in favor of the former. The occupant is simply forced to fit." James Marston Fitch, *American Building: 1: The Historical Forces That Shaped It* (Boston: Houghton Mifflin Co., 1966), Second edition, p. 314.

[85] John R. Myer, in *Planning for Diversity and Choice,* Stanford Anderson, editor (Cambridge: M.I.T. Press, 1968), p. 294.

relationships between man and environment and decide which are important and testable, because environmental designers are unlikely to. Their traditions stand too far from science for that.[86] Because they have seen so many variables as equally important, architects' own research literature is scanty. "Systems analysis" appeals to environmentalists partly because it saves them from having to limit their generalist, and too often amorphous, outlook.

Merely to increase the number of things the architect must take into account without . . . any limit as to what he can manipulate at one time, I think, is trivial. . . . The holistic view is a mistake not because it's wrong but because it's not possible to implement. You ought to be concerned with intelligent ways of limiting yourself.[87]

The interest in design programming, for example, has been more an expansion of a technical vocabulary and less an addition of explanations of relationships between man and environment. The resistance within environmental design—and again, especially architecture—to explictness of intention is so considerable that unless the human sciences find a more natural entrance into environmental design issues than they have now, research into basic questions will continue to be stymied and obscured.[88]

[86] "Within the last ten years there have been less than 350 architects who have been or are now involved in research to some degree . . . somewhat less than 1% of the registered architects in this country are active in research. . . . The 49 agencies [universities, centers, and institutes] covered list research projects over the last 8 years involving just over $5 million . . . $½ million per year for the entire profession." Benjamin H. Evans, *AIA Research Survey* (Washington: American Institute of Architects, April 1965), p. iv.

[87] Aaron Fleisher, in *Planning for Diversity and Choice,* Anderson, editor, p. 296. Fleisher is trained in the natural sciences, as a metereologist, and is an Associate Professor of City and Regional Planning at M.I.T.

[88] Christopher Alexander says, "there are many designers who . . . insist that design must be a purely intuitive process: that it is hopeless to try and understand it sensibly because its problems are too deep. . . . Enormous resistance to the idea of systematic processes of design is coming from people who recognize correctly the importance of intuition, but then make a fetish of it which excludes the possibility of asking reasonable questions. . . . We must face the fact that we are on the brink of times when man may be able to magnify his intellectual and inventive capability, just as in the nineteenth century he used machines to magnify his physical capacity." *Notes on the Synthesis of Form,* pp. 8–10. Christian Norberg-Schulz says, "Let us hope that modern architecture has contributed to solve essential human problems. The actual situation, however, makes us understand that the solutions are still rather defective, not least because of the omission of fundamental and symbolical factors. We must realize that the main responsibility for this state of affairs is the architects' own. Our highly complicated new world demands new professional methods, but . . . the architect has isolated himself

Still another reason for urgency: systems analysis and operations research are on the verge of becoming pivotal for urban policy. We must be on our guard to prevent their domination without distinguishing the substantive questions that are always involved; the content should be inspiring the method, not the other way round. The human sciences should be helping to unearth values, customs, and priorities, and in environmental design we are already far behind. Distressingly, for example, Mumford has raised objections to the proposed relief of severe housing shortages in cities by using industrialized building technology. He reads the mode of this technology's use as the only mode he, or any of us, knows from its history to date: the technician and the technical means decide the goals as well.[89] But if industrialized housing were designed from the start to embody what people expect of their living environment, then we would all have a great deal less to fear.

Finally, this formulation noticeably deemphasizes those aspects of a "satisfying" environment most usually spoken of: the visual quality of the built environment, and attention to people's preferences and tastes.[90] The natural synthesis of enacted be-

and clung to obsolete ideas and methods. Often he still supports the romantic nineteenth century idea that the artist should only express his autonomous personality." *Intentions in Architecture*, p. 20. Christopher Gotch, in *Work: Twenty Personal Accounts, Volume 2:* "I became an architect because the appearance of buildings held my interest. . . . Architecture was basically a visual matter with the utilitarian concept secondary. It never crossed my mind that there might be a social content. At least, no one ever mentioned it . . . that the visual is undoubtedly secondary to technique and economy has been a shock, compensated somewhat by the belated discovery that architecture is not just a design process in a vacuum, but one ineradicably associated with people. This sounds incredibly naive. But then my own background reflects the cocoon in which so many of us are imprisoned." Pp. 147–148, 155.

89 "With fifty billion dollars as bait, a new kind of Aerospace Industry would move in, with all its typical paraphernalia of scientific research and engineering design. At that moment your plans for creating humanly satisfactory neighborhoods would go up in smoke. 'General Space Housing, Incorporated' will solve your housing problem, swiftly and efficiently, though not painlessly, by following their own typical method, derived from the ancient Pyramid Builders: eliminate the human factor by enforcing mechanical conformity and imposing automatic obedience. With the aid of their systems analyzers and computers, these high-powered organizations would design housing units even more prisonlike in character than those we now have." Lewis Mumford, *The Urban Prospect* (London: Secker & Warburg, 1968), pp. 225–226.

90 "One central reason for the drop in urban amenity is due to the fact that architects and urbanists alike persist in regarding the city as a largely visual phenomenon. Urban design is envisioned as being primarily a process

havior with the visual quality of environment—for perception is also behavioral—is taken apart here only to raise other issues not so well understood. A resurgence of valuing the natural landscape, landmarks of old, green oases in stark urban settings, and the ensemble of street architecture has been with us for several years now, and many scholars and practitioners in design are continuing to contribute concepts and methods that will help to create beautiful and more congruent environments.[91] The process advocated here should move us, as we urgently need to be moved, toward ways of quantifying what are usually considered intangibles, including aesthetics: if we can document only the defects of the visual environment, then those are the only defects we are likely to remedy. And visual defects can readily be documented in pictures; a whole literature of illustrated books on visual assets and deficits has established itself in the last several years.[92]

of pictorial or plastic manipulation. As a result, the multidimensioned, psychosomatic reality of social life is violated by formalistic, two-dimensional designing." Fitch, *American Building*, p. 282.

[91] Denise Scott Brown, "Team 10, Perspecta 10, and the Present State of Architectural Theory," *Journal of the American Institute of Planners*, Vol. 33, No. 1, January 1967, pp. 42–49; John Gulick, "Images of an Arab City," *Journal of the American Institute of Planners*, Vol. 29, No. 3, August 1963, pp. 179–198; Carl Steinitz, "Meaning and the Congruence of Urban Form and Activity," *Journal of the American Institute of Planners*, Vol. 34, No. 4, July 1968, pp. 233–248; Rai Y. Okamoto and Frank E. Williams, *Urban Design Manhattan* (New York: Viking Press for The Regional Plan Association, 1969); Derk de Jonge, "Applied Hodology," *Landscape*, Vol. 17, No. 2, Winter 1967–68, pp. 10–11; Robert Kates, "The Pursuit of Beauty in the Environment," *Landscape*, Vol. 16. No. 2, Winter 1966–67, pp. 21–25; Françoise Choay, "Urbanism and Semiology," in *Meaning in Architecture*, Charles Jencks and George Baird, editors (New York: George Braziller, 1970), pp. 26–37.

[92] Three having classic impact are: Christopher Tunnard and Boris Pushkarev, *Man-Made America: Chaos or Control?* (New Haven: Yale University Press, 1963); Ian Nairn, *The American Landscape: A Critical View* (New York: Random House, 1965); and Peter Blake, *God's Own Junkyard: The Planned Deterioration of America's Landscape* (New York: Holt, Rinehart, and Winston, 1964). J. B. Jackson, for many years editor of *Landscape*, a rich source of leading-edge formulations, discusses works of this genre for the side of the coin being taken up here: "works of landscape or urban art— parks, parkways gardens; civic centers and formal squares and avenues—conceived in these terms are likely to be both beautiful and useful. But we come back once more to the issue of design in terms of spectator art versus design in terms of livability, and the preservationist is constitutionally unable to design in terms of changing patterns of use. He provides us with the experience of extraordinary beauty, he makes it possible for us to step out of the everyday world; but he does nothing to make that everyday world more livable." "Limited Access," *Landscape*, Vol. 14, No. 1, August 1964, p. 23.

It can certainly be anticipated that there will be overlap between what the resources in an environment mean in my terms and those criteria used for visual and perceptual satisfactions. Many rubrics of "good design" are based on customary behavioral expectations. A path system in a housing development that meets behavioral expectations of various kinds may also be a formal property that brings order and harmony to the location of buildings and to the visual experience of being in the environment.[93]

Work is going apace in psychology and sociology to refine the techniques for reliably evoking statements of preferences about colors, acoustics, room arrangements, details of landscape.[94] In developing data for a situation where a "majority opinion" is decisive, as in a community group faced with alternative designs for a building facade, or where the characteristics and preferences of a homogenous group of users need to be uncovered, those techniques will be valuable to client and designer.

But on the whole, seeking to satisfy opinion and preference is

[93] In an essay sharing the idea of environment as enabling and supportive, Carr has speculated about criteria for environmental forms which might properly be termed resources; although he cautions at the same time that these criteria are "more in the nature of hypotheses than design tools at the moment," they deserve use. For example, "stimulate and facilitate exploration of the environment . . . enhance the unique qualities of environmental settings . . . increase the plasticity and manipulability of city form to the actions of small groups and individuals . . . adapt the form of environmental settings to facilitate the predominant plans being executed within them." Stephen Carr, "The City of the Mind," in *Environment for Man*, William R. Ewald, Jr., editor (Bloomington: Indiana University Press, 1967), pp. 219–223.

[94] Kenneth H. Craik, "The Comprehension of the Everyday Physical Environment," *Journal of the American Institute of Planners*, Vol. 34, No. 1, January 1968, pp. 29–37; idem., "Human Responsiveness to Landscape: An Environmental Psychological Perspective," *Student Publication of the School of Design*, North Carolina State University, 1968; idem., "Assessing Environmental Dispositions," paper presented at the annual meeting of the American Psychological Association, Washington, D.C., September 1969; Arne S. Dolven, "Reactions to Hypothetical and Actual Job and House Lot Choice," *Journal of the American Institute of Planners*, Vol. 34, No. 3, May 1968, pp. 189–191; John B. Lansing and Robert W. Marans, "Evaluation of Neighborhood Quality," *Journal of the American Institute of Planners*, Vol. 35, No. 3, May 1969, pp. 195–199; William Michelson, "An Empirical Analysis of Urban Environmental Preferences," *Journal of the American Institute of Planners*, Vol. 32, No. 6, November 1966, pp. 355–360, and "Urban Sociology as an Aid to Urban Physical Development: Some Research Strategies," *Journal of the American Institute of Planners*, Vol. 34, No. 2, March 1968, pp. 105–108; Amos Rapoport and Robert E. Kantor, "Complexity and Ambiguity in Environmental Design," *Journal of the American Institute of Planners*, Vol. 33, No. 4, July 1967, pp. 210–221.

the one means we have now for involving the ultimate user in design process. I believe it to be a constricted means of authentic involvement for him and a sterile means for the designer in responding to him in a real and rich way. To permit the designer to meet the original and fundamental problem that he faces, that of allocating space and paying heed to the inhabitants' often conflicting priorities, it is not the preference structure of people that ought to cast imperatives, but rather their behavior structure.[95] As suggested earlier, when the question put to the user asks him to describe his purposes and the means available for achieving them, he will be more likely to have ideas about missing or alternative means than he will be likely to have abstract preferences for what he has no experience of. The designer has rights too: his "behavioral" satisfactions come from exercising his imagination and creating anew out of a wider understanding of design possibilities than the layman has, and it is inappropriate to put his well-worked ideas about physical forms to a test of preference in the abstract.

"If anyone will tell us architects what people need, we'll tell them how to build it. We can only reflect what civilization and what culture we have," said Mies van der Rohe, to whom no one seems ever to have said what they need; and so he maintained his prerogative to build for himself.[96] That prerogative expresses a view of power over environment that is passing: the unified plan, the single idea carried out to perfection—whether a Mies building or cities like Washington or St. Petersburg—is always a manifestation of unshared power.

The revolution in environmental design I am calling for is meant to put an end to that view of power in a process where it has been questioned very little at the points where it matters very much. On a visit to each of the Scandinavian countries, talking with architects, planners, and sociologists, I soon found that they would not accept my compliments on their responsive and humane buildings and towns, turning them away with expressions of considerable dissatisfaction with the process bringing them about: as they saw it, the decisions were made by too

95 Elaine Frieden has discussed the limitations of "simple statements of preference" in a study of the kind of housing that would meet the behavioral needs of the elderly, in "Social Differences and Housing for the Aged," *Journal of the American Institute of Planners,* Vol. 26, No. 2, May 1960, pp. 119–124.
96 Wolf Von Eckardt, *A Place To Live* (New York: Delacorte Press, 1967), pp. 89–90.

few with too little discussion about the location of new towns, the composition of the housing stock, the mixture of land uses, the provision of community facilities. They were in ferment about wider participation and disclosure. The same is happening in Great Britain, just now, after years of creating New Towns and a domestic architecture worthy of emulation, where the issue of decentralization of decisionmaking has begun to reach a crescendo.[97] And so even though people may come to see that the product is the least of it—that one gets a road or building anyway, in the end—their ability to enter into the process is limited by its own definition. Defining the process differently will itself be the revolution.

[97] Ministry of Housing and Local Government, *People and Planning: Report of the Committee on Public Participation in Planning* (Skeffington Committee) (London: HMSO, 1969), 71 pp. See also Maurice Broady, "The Social Context of Urban Planning," in *Planning for People* (London: Bedford Square Press of the National Council of Social Service, 1968), pp. 99–117.

3
The Designer's Intentions
Toward Man

Current Intentions

We have then, a background of criticism of buildings based on building science and technology, and a background of criticism of buildings as individual cultural artifacts and not too much in between. The gap is filled with common sense. . . . Common sense and experience, and this is what worries me. . . . In my experience the crucial aspect of criticism of students' work centres around the question "does it work." This question has a bluff, down-to-earth sound, but it is not necessarily capable of a precise answer. It may be easy to answer, on the evidence available, when it is applied to a technical matter like a damp-proof course, or a formal matter like a game of symmetry. But it is not so simple when it is applied to a question of use. It then presupposes an attempt to interpret drawings as representative of operational relationships. We look at plans and we imagine doors swinging, drawers being pulled, corridors full of racing feet, people falling down unexpected steps or jamming on landings. We compare the drawings with similar drawings or with actual buildings in our memory store and we say, with considerable confidence, it wouldn't work, the circulations would cross, the corridor is too narrow, the room is claustrophobic, the wcs are too far away, the waiting space is intimidating, and so on.

In other words, we attribute to the drawings or models operational qualities based on our own experience, and assess the performance which we would expect, imagining the building built and us in it. I think we all know, privately, what a dicey kind of criticism this can be. . . . It is hardly surprising that in so many cases students have become sceptical of our opinions and of our evaluations. . . .[1]

And so, Maxwell is saying, we lack a way of matching in our imaginations a pattern of form to a pattern of use. It is for this very reason that the definition of the user's expectations about his behavior is essential: in order to get substance into the creative act where there is now merely the personal attribution of the designer. Without this substance to use in explaining his work, the designer can state only his intentions toward the formal and geometric qualities of space, not his intentions toward man in it. Without such substance, the designer reverts to the pathetic fallacy.

Several designers have been developing techniques for uncovering both demographic and behavioral attributes of users, and trying, generally, to state more about people that their subsequent designs should respond to. Duffy has outlined a method for mapping employee relationships in a bank and in a lawyer's

---

1 Robert Maxwell, "Work Criticism Methods," Conference of University Schools of Architecture, Cambridge, England, April 1967, pp. 8–9.

office, concentrating particularly on the mode of the display.[2] Alexander and Poyner identify conflicts between physical arrangements and people's "tendencies"—to be "resolved" by a "relation . . . a geometric arrangement which prevents a conflict."[3] Alexander's end product generally includes both the method and the design idea it gives rise to as one and the same thing, exemplified in the "pattern language" where the physical design arrived at for a particularly well-explained situation is meant to become a prototype for use in any other similar situation.[4] Brill is developing methods for gaining data from the client on his priorities for nine environmental performance characteristics which describe the qualities of various rooms for the kinds of activities they will house.[5]

Other designers are coming to user requirements by a still different approach, trying to overcome the sterility for designing when the properties of the environment are described instead of the properties of the users. Spring states user requirements in a sentence structure meant to insure that the user's needs are uppermost: "All residents should be able to reach public transportation within 5 minutes of their home."[6] Field has tried also to keep separate "the activity process" and the "spatial environment" in programming a pediatric hospital. "We were initially determined to disregard spatial considerations as part of our analysis of work. The results of the analysis gave us a sense of the elbowroom required rather than square feet standards. . . . We were interested in qualitative matters of basic configuration and pattern." Field's user requirements are stated as what he terms "Design Directives" intended to inform the architect and to have a "bearing" on the ultimate design.[7] Van der Ryn's research

2 Francis Duffy, "A Method of Analysing and Charting Relationships in the Office," *The Architects' Journal*, 12 March 1969, pp. 693–699.
3 Christopher Alexander and Barry Poyner, "The Atoms of Environmental Structure," Ministry of Public Buildings and Works, London, 1966.
4 Christopher Alexander, Sara Ishikawa, Murray Silverstein, *A Pattern Language That Generates Multi-Service Centers* (Berkeley: Center for Environmental Structure, 1968); Christopher Alexander, Sara Ishikawa, Sanford Hirshen, Shlomo Angel, and Christie Coffin, *Houses Generated by Patterns* (Berkeley: Center for Environmental Structure, 1969).
5 Michael Brill, "A Systems Approach to Environmental Design," *Environment*, January 1970, pp. 38–41.
6 Bernard P. Spring, "Criteria for Housing Design Evaluation (Draft)," School of Architecture, Princeton University, mimeo, 9 pp., no date.
7 Hermann H. Field, "Report on Interdisciplinary Research in Hospital Design at the Tufts-New England Medical Center in Boston," AIA Architectural Research Conference, October 21, 1966, St. Louis, pp. 2–3.

on dormitory occupants is both user-evaluation and criteria for future dormitory design; he suggests a prototype design answering the difficulties students found.[8]

In a similar vein, Brolin (architect) and Zeisel (sociologist) have shown the user requirements that can be obtained with systematic research, by using *The Urban Villagers*—Herbert Gans's study of working-class Italian life in Boston's West End—as though it were the research for a design program.[9] They wrote an illustrative program which used the North End as the locus, choosing only Gans's data on social behavior. Their syntax for stating user requirements led to design proposals for house and site layouts. They found that of the observations Gans made that they could translate to form, these attributes were present: a primary actor and his activity, the significant others in the situation, and the relationship stated between the primary actor and the significant others. The inclusion and exclusion of people defined the spatial connection or separation, but the authors are careful to stress that their verbal requirements "define a minimum set of social behavior patterns which the physical structure should not prohibit" and in no way limit the responses the designer creates.

Observation: When there are guests the men separate from the women by going into the living room. Men and women often stay apart the entire evening. Even at the kitchen table, men will stay at one end and women at the other.

Requirement: Privacy between men's and women's social gathering areas.

Observation: West Enders have a different sense of privacy than middle-class families. They do not mind the crowded tenements if they do not have to climb many stairs.

Requirement: Maximum connection between apartments.[10]

Zeisel reports another study he and Brolin have made of about twelve Puerto Rican families living in tenements which were to be renovated:

We talked with them about what they liked and disliked in their apartments as they were . . . about what they would like in new apartments, about what they did in the apartments, and about how they spent their day. We also showed them schematic diagrams of different apartment layouts and asked them to choose one and explain why. . . . At the same time we noted

8 Sim Van Der Ryn and Murray Silverstein, "Berkeley: How Do Students Really Live?" *Architectural Forum*, July-August 1967, pp. 91–97.
9 Brent C. Brolin and John Zeisel, "Mass Housing: Social Research and Design," *Architectural Forum*, July-August 1968, pp. 66–70.
10 Ibid., p. 5.

where people were when we came in, what they did while we were there, and who else came in. We noted the physical attributes of the apartments: furniture placement, wall decorations and any changes the tenants made in their apartments. We looked for physical cues of use, misuse, changing of apartments, non-use, and of what a room or a space meant to the tenant.[11]

Their physical design took into account what they had observed; and then they compared their design ideas with those of still another architect who was familiar with the tenants, but "followed only one set of standards: what he, himself—a middle-class white American—would like, given the income limitations."

The living-dining room area in this plan is one large undifferentiated space. The possibility of the family splitting into two groups as our study showed was needed, would be practically impossible. . . . The kitchen could not serve as a lock or turnstile —another requirement. None of the kitchens have windows facing onto the street. Communication would be impossible. . . . There is no sacred space. Although the layout of the apartments might seem compatible to many, it conflicts with the majority of the requirements found during our study of low-income Puerto Ricans in East Harlem.[12]

The value and promise of these designers' work are in their attention to empirical facts—the behavioral expectations of the users—which they are willing to let guide design inductively. Even so, they do not invoke a theory of human nature for environmental design to explain why some data are sought and not others. Some of this work makes assertions about the inhabitants' needs solely as a matter of personal conviction. Designers have directed the research, not human scientists, and few efforts have even included them. Although designers try their best when they try at all, current programming demonstrates on the whole the emptiness of the unworked terrain between the human sciences and design. When people are thought about during the conception of a new environment, the result is that not nearly enough of what it is possible to think about them is brought to bear. In an appendix I have recorded an exercise illustrating the scope of the designer's vocabulary when he thinks about what people need from their environment.

One traditional influence in environmental design—and one which uses as little empirical knowledge as possible about man

11 John Zeisel, "Symbolic Meaning of Space and Physical Dimension of Social Relations," Paper presented at the American Sociological Association, September 1969, San Francisco, pp. 2–3.
12 Ibid., p. 5.

—is the pleasant dreaming up of utopias. The idealizing they express is a condensation of only our best selves, an often childish image of only the good that lies within us, to the exclusion of what is not thought so.[13] Some critics have suggested that the absence of the idea of "original sin" characterizes utopias, so in utopianism, as in light music, only nobility, purity, and bursting optimism are displayed. Surely these are indeed ours in life, but they are not all that is ours, as the anti-utopian writers have tried to point out.[14] Serious music works its way into and out of conflict, toward a resolution satisfying largely because a complexity lingers even after the finale. Utopian society is of necessity a simplification of complexity devised so that we might be able to comprehend what is really not comprehensible. And so people bring more to the places they inhabit—and expect more—than the utopian tradition can stimulate the environmental designer to think about. Left to himself, his articulation of what is human now depends on chance and personal awareness: how profoundly he is capable of thinking about people —some from his training, some from maturity of insight, some from his prejudices and opinions.

Hassid has analyzed the criteria used by architectural "juries" —panels of teachers and critics who evaluate the work of students and of architectural competitions. Out of forty-five categories of criteria, two relate directly to the "emotional and physical demands of the human." The table shows the frequency with which these two criteria are mentioned relative to all other criteria, classified according to the occupation of the jury member.[15]

13 "The complacency, rigidity, and lack of opportunity for deviant behavior that characterized the utopias of the emerging industrial civilization persisted in those of the twentieth century. . . . Since there appears to be little demand for utopia, since no one for a generation has produced social or physicial-design utopias of importance, and since utopias are caricatures anyway, this essay amounts to an epitaph—but an epitaph only for the rigid social and physical utopias of the past, for utopia as a product, and not for utopia as a process for clarifying policy, particularly in city planning." Martin Meyerson, "Utopian Traditions and the Planning of Cities," in *The Future Metropolis,* edited by Lloyd Rodwin (New York: George Braziller, 1961), pp. 243 and 247.
14 David Lodge, "Utopia and Criticism: The Radical Longing for Paradise," *Encounter,* April 1969, pp. 65–75.
15 Sami Hassid, "Development and Application of a System for Recording Critical Evaluation of Architectural Works," College of Environmental Design, University of California, Berkeley, July 1964, 37 pp. A first-time effort to regularize the criteria of the jury-system is Educational Testing Service,

| | Number of Criteria out of 45 Discussed More Often than | |
Critic's Occupation	Emotional Demands	Physical Demands
Architect	12	33
Architectural critic	25	34
Structural engineer	26	30
Designer	35	19
Periodical reporter	7	24
Architectural educator	19	30

One very likely reason why both the "emotional and physical demands" are so much less discussed than structural and technical aspects is that there is an inadequate vocabulary for doing so.

The Equilibrating Model That Is Man

The environments designed for the elderly, for children, the ill, the handicapped may seem to stand simply as examples of what can be done generally. We are used to thinking that studying extremity can help us to understand the ordinary. But in reality it seems to end there—extrapolations are not made to environments for people who are visibly fit, capable, and adult. And yet they may still be distressed by their environments. I have been suggesting that their ordinariness lies in their daily round and the resources appropriate to it which in turn depend on how attributes like ethnicity, social class, educational attainment combine into diverse behavioral expectations.

Still another realm of human attributes must be acknowledged: Why does man do what he does, as he moves through the many behavior streams and circuits of his twenty-four hours, the seasons of the year, and the arcs of his life-span? What is it he is expressing in visible behaviors? What is he doing it for? Human purpose, as we come to think through the processes of conceiving a new environment, has two separable dimensions: one is enacted, visible, and purposive behavior; the other is the reason for undertaking the behavior in the first place. When environmental design considers both dimensions fully, we will, I believe, see new buildings and neighborhoods, spaces and forms, that we do not know of today.

A Handbook for Measurement and Evaluation in Design Education (Washington: American Institute of Architects, August 1969).

Together these dimensions shape a theory of human nature for environmental design, meant to help the designer to explain his intentions toward man in terms of their consequences: what people will find in the environments they inhabit that reflects what they know of themselves and of their reasons for being there. The opportunities and resources they find will cost money to create, to be sure, but until we can specify the human cost of not having them we will lose arguments to heighten their priority among the always-present competitors with "hard" economic documentation.[16]

The essential mediating term belonging in a theory of human nature for environmental design is the striving of people for equilibrium in the various realms of their personal and social life, toward that which maintains and extends their sense of competence and self-esteem. We have been very quick to adopt a "natural systems" or "organic" model to describe social organization or invisible economic and spatial networks—but how we shrink from so describing man himself! He is just that: a living, breathing, homeostatic, natural system. It is time indeed to get our metaphors straight: we are the original system striving to stay in equilibrium; the model lives!

My Name is Legion: Foundations for a Theory of Man in Relation to Culture by Alexander H. Leighton is a contemporary work in the human sciences offering a natural framework for human studies in environmental design.[17] The book discusses ideas about human nature and personality, eventually used in research into the mental health of members of a community.[18]

16 "The price paid in adapting to uncongenial environments may be difficult to estimate in money, sickness, inefficiency, and turnover, but it is too high if we can design congenial environments for the same money or less." Robert Sommer, *Personal Space: The Behavioral Basis of Design* (Englewood Cliffs, N.J.: Prentice-Hall, 1969), p. 171. A sociologist makes the point that the "nonconforming usage" brought on by the Pullman kitchen, efficient for no one, or picture windows always covered for privacy means that the facilities people would make use of are missing—a sheer waste built in. Irving Rosow, "The Social Effects of the Physical Environment, *Journal of the American Institute of Planners,* Vol. 27, No. 2, May 1961, p. 128.

17 Alexander H. Leighton, *My Name is Legion: Foundations for a Theory of Man in Relation to Culture, Volume I of The Stirling County Study of Psychiatric Disorder and Sociocultural Environment* (New York: Basic Books, 1959).

18 Charles C. Hughes, Marc-Adélard Tremblay, Robert N. Rapoport, and Alexander H. Leighton, *People of Cove and Woodlot: Communities from the Viewpoint of Social Psychiatry (Volume II)* and Dorothea C. Leighton, John S. Harding, David B. Macklin, Allister M. Macmillan, and Alexander H. Leighton, *The Character of Danger: Psychiatric Symptoms in Selected Com-*

Leighton, a psychiatrist, has developed the term "essential striv-ing sentiments" for representing what personality is. Sentiment unites the otherwise mutually exclusive meanings of cognition and affect, and in Leighton's careful argument, the sentiments are juxtaposed with the idea of the human being in a state of striving, in order to maintain and find psychical equilibrium. It is a usage appealing for a theory of human nature for environ-mental design because it allows the ensemble of environment to become related to the ensemble of human behavior when both are observed at a personal scale.

The "essential striving sentiments" each represent a clustering of human tendencies, basic urges, affects, drives, and instincts. Leighton makes no special claim for the ten he has named—calling them just "convenient handles"—and for my purpose here, they stand usefully enough as is: they illustrate categories of behavioral data we should be collecting in parallel with the demographic data we are accustomed to seek. The studies made during the inception phase to uncover a population's behavioral expectations should try to identify the behavior streams and circuits within each of these clusterings, joining in that way the questions "what people do and why."

Physical security

Sexual satisfaction

The expression of hostility

The expression of love

The securing of love

The securing of recognition

The expression of spontaneity (called variously positive force, creativity, volition)

Orientation in terms of one's place in society and the places of others

The securing and maintaining of membership in a definite hu-man group

A sense of belonging to a moral order and being right in what one does, being in and of a system of values

Sentiments, therefore, provide a framework in terms of which personalities may be characterized descriptively and then salient points explored and analyzed with reference to origins and deter-minants. Sentiments are convenient handles with which to grasp the complex system and at the same time constitute crucial as-pects of what is meant by personality. Schematically, one may

munities (Volume III) of the Stirling County Study of Psychiatric Disorder and Sociocultural Environment (New York: Basic Books, 1960).

picture personality as a sphere, the surface of which, interacting with the environment, is composed of sentiments. Below this surface and contributing to it are basic urges and unconscious processes . . . personality is the functioning of a self-integrating unit of sentiments, and the essence of its functioning is resistance to dissolution while moving through sequential changes along a life-arc.[19]

The extensive criticism of high-rise apartment buildings as an appropriate environment for raising children might be reexamined in these terms as a practical measure—especially because so many public housing projects are high-rise and will continue in use for many years to come. Perhaps they can be remodeled. Let us assume that in the studies made for the design program behavioral expectations and behavior streams and circuits are sought within each of the essential striving sentiments. The studies suggest that the present physical environment is deficient mainly with respect to the mothers' strivings to express love and concern for their children, their wish to trust themselves and others, and their identity of role as mother. We can ask—within the imaginary bounds of this imaginary inquiry—what kinds of environmental modifications might compensate and reinforce these strivings? Perhaps the first few floors of all buildings should be made into apartments for families with young children, with access to ground play space from each dwelling unit. Or instead of physical rehabilitation, perhaps funds should be spent on a crew of helpers who supervise play groups on every other floor and care for children outdoors.

Whatever the responses to the problem, they have begun to unfold by reference to the behavior the mothers want to exhibit for which the environment provides no assets. In this way, we may see both physical forms and kinds of jobs unknown before. As we rediscover that there are many links between fulfilled behavior and the physical environment that are forged only if a person intervenes, we will also be discovering new kinds of urban services that can be said to be essential. Their lack becomes measurable.

It is also possible to use the essential striving sentiments as a framework for criticizing the built environment in use, to widen the kinds of lessons we learn. I have analyzed a play space for children by translating the ten sentiments into my idea of what they might mean to children using it and evaluated the extent

[19] Leighton, *My Name is Legion*, pp. 27–28.

to which the environmental resources meet the expectations children are likely to have.

Small children's play area, about thirty feet by forty-five feet, abutting an eight-story apartment building. The persons expected to use it are adult women or other child caretakers, and children from infancy to about eight years old.

The play space as a whole does not have either equipment or separations of interior areas that relate to age gradients. The adults taking care of the children playing there have no place to sit. For children of these ages, close absorption in play may cause forgetfulness of bladder control, but no ground-floor toilets are provided. Another missing resource is a digging spot or sandbox: outdoor play is qualitatively different from indoor play and the handling of earth in some form or other signifies "outdoors."

The problem of the noise generated by children's play areas vis-à-vis the surrounding houses is exacerbated by siting it behind the building instead of on the street side where the children's noises would blend with traffic noises and probably for the most part be drowned out. The adult caretakers might also expect to see and chat with neighbors passing by. The siting as a whole is negative not only to the naturally noisy expressions of children at play, but to their expression of spontaneity, their feeling of being welcome as they are in society, and the probability that they would be cautioned or chastized by parents or other adults for simply being themselves.

My translation of what each sentiment might mean to children of these ages and my evaluation of the resource appear in parentheses on the next page.

The inventive resources currently being included in other children's play spaces have acknowledged an expanded range of understandings about children's maturation processes and their imaginative capabilities.[20] That expanded range is the literature of the last fifty years in psychology, physiology, pediatrics, and education brought into the designer's work at his drawing board, not as any final truth about children, but, more intelligently, as illuminating to many of the variables he can control.

And so, besides the new terms "assets" and "deficits" made possible by the concepts of behavioral expectations and behavior circuits, a widened recognition of what man is about leads to

[20] See, for example, Richard Dattner, *Design for Play* (New York: Van Nostrand Reinhold Co., 1969).

Essential Striving Sentiment	Relevant Resource
Physical security (safety from cars on parking lot; dogs; wandering and getting lost; protection from one's own immaturity)	4-foot high cyclone wire fence (relates positively)
Sexual satisfaction (play materials and forms that offer tactile and motor activities related to body awareness; sexual identity; and pleasurable muscular feelings)	Slide, swings (relates positively)
Expression of hostility (shouting, competitive play, digging, destroying, taking apart objects)	Playspace abuts building (relates negatively)
Expression of love (cooperative play)	Individual-use play equipment; waiting for turns (relates negatively)
Securing of love Securing of recognition (gaining adult approval)	Entire site relates negatively; playspace offers little opportunity for children to create and take pride in games or building of forms that can bring self-recognition
Expression of spontaneity (thinking up new games)	Fixed play elements whose use is limited (relates negatively)
Orientation of place in society and places of others (looking around now and then)	Site is tucked behind the building instead of sharing in the active passers-by movement
Securing and maintaining membership in a definite human group	Site is discontinuous with life around it (relates negatively)
Sense of belonging to a moral order	The siting of the building's parking lot, which gets better sun all day, has shade trees and a view toward a pleasant residential street, symbolizes all too well the priority for society of car storage over play space

still another vocabulary for criticism. The extent to which the physical resource succeeds in its relationship to any of the essential striving sentiments can be expressed on a scale of this kind:

preservative: that resource which maintains or reinforces the essential striving sentiments and life itself

affirmative: that resource which supports strivings toward the next stage of development, expanded role, deepening of capabilities, confirmation of achievement, acknowledgment of individuality, increased competence

destructive: that resource which fails out of insufficiency to be either preservative or affirmative because it actively inhibits or does not have either a preservative or affirmative relationship.

The continuum is primitively subjective now, meant to clarify our righteous indignations; it could eventually shape questions for orthodox research.

The continuum should frame the designer's explanations of what he creates in response to the design program. The resources most likely to be termed preservative are those minima we have come to write into fire codes, building regulations, and sanitary codes to protect life and health. The resources we would judge to be affirmative are those with great spiritual content—churches, opera houses, monuments, oases like Paley Park and Boston's Public Garden—and those less obvious (and less frequent) like schools for creative learning, pedestrian precincts, clear transit maps and signs—all those elements which recognize individuality and competence—termed now, weakly, amenities.

The resources that are absent or insufficient are destructive: the traffic light missing from the busy intersection is not simply absent, it is actively destructive. When there is insufficient space in the apartment for the piano the family wants or the sewing paraphernalia for making the family clothes or a quiet place to read, the resource is not simply missing: the lack of sufficient space is actively destructive to strivings for self-fulfillment. At this end of the scale lies the captivity of narrow options.

These new terms for our critical and explanatory vocabulary could mobilize the revolutionary aspirations of environmental design, not quite so established in fact as Mrs. Huxtable's eloquence would have us believe.

What has taken place, essentially, is a revolution in the philosophy and practice of architecture today. . . . It is a revolution in the understanding of the nature and consequences of what is built everywhere, on everyone; the manner in which construction solves or exacerbates human problems and diminishes or increases the human spirit. . . . Depending on one's degree of conscience and breadth of overview, some building can even be interpreted as a crime against society—a crime for which there are not only no penalties, but which carries the rewards of tax shelters. Today, architecture, too, has been "radicalized."[21]

The insights of the human sciences about human nature in all its guises should be used, then, not to "specify" environments and behavioral "outputs"—the kind of certainty that belongs

21 Ada Louise Huxtable, "Seen Any Good Buildings Lately?," *The New York Times*, January 11, 1970, Section 2, p. 25.

only to extremity—but rather, to evoke for the designer a far more realistic and wider vocabulary of the human expectations there are. How he might make his response to a design program that limns people in such widened terms is the next question. He will have the new opportunity of using his enormously inventive capacities toward human purposes and strivings he may never have known existed. The technical and material innovations he now manipulates into arid futuristic and pop architecture, in paper projects never built, may suddenly be capable of an authentic *raison d'être* in human terms.

The Dramatic Analogy in Design

The question of method in design—those operations the designer must perform in order to make the leap from what people need to what he puts in place for them to use—cannot be "answered" but must instead be constantly explored. Alexander's *Notes on the Synthesis of Form* was a milestone in design method, offering a well-worked alternative to the "unreliable" intuition of the designer.[22] The idea of explicitness is penetrating environmental design, relying on analysis and synthesis and the hardware they can command,[23] but the appropriate vocabulary in which to be explicit has not yet been found. The operations of the equation—whether to add, substract, multiply, or divide—seem to be settled before the values of the terms they manipulate have been stated.

The dominant metaphor in design methodology is, in fact, mathematical, where a new environment is created at the drawing board as a "solution to a problem." The metaphor carries a basic misreading of man's efforts: he sets in motion ways of dealing with change, conflict, tomorrow—and he retains his freedom to redirect these efforts so that if one way does not seem to make a significant difference, another is begun. It is the movement of life through its own continuum that environmental design should be relating to. If the human striving to move from one point to the next with adequacy, with grace,

[22] "In present design practice, this critical step, during which the problem is prepared and translated into design, always depends on some kind of intuition. Though design is by nature imaginative and intuitive, and we could easily trust it if the designer's intuition were reliable, as it is it inspires very little confidence." Christopher Alexander, *Notes on the Synthesis of Form* (Cambridge: Harvard University Press, 1967), p. 77.

[23] The *Design Methods Group Newsletter* is published 10 times a year, sponsored by the College of Environmental Design, University of California, Berkeley and the Department of Architecture, Washington University, St. Louis.

with recognition is what the work of the world is all about, then the measurement of social disorganization by statistics on death rates or crime or disease is the ultimate proof of the impoverishment of our culture's vocabulary: preventable death and the extremities of disease occur when the points along the continuum that maintain life and fulfillment have failed to do so. Those are the rates of disorganization we should be measuring—where there are known deficits to the maintenance of known human needs. We should not be counting the numbers of people in a state of malnutrition without also counting the numbers of opportunities to feed them not taken.

Because real solutions are so very hard to come by in the real and capricious world, the emphasis on them is a kind of bravado, a whistling in the dark to keep up our spirits. Even though failure and low spirits are inevitable within the confines of the metaphor, it continues to be elaborated: fit and misfit, conflict and resolution, correlation and prediction are the terms controlling the designer's definition and evaluation of what he does. But if not "rules" and matchings, then what vocabulary better expresses the relation between animate people and inanimate environment as the designer explains what he is trying to accomplish?

To find it, our subject needs first to be recognized as inherently ambiguous. Kris suggests that our language for thinking about ambiguity may give us false impressions of the differences between scientific precision and poetry.

The distinction of these various types of ambiguity suggests that the common dualism between scientific and poetic language . . . has been overemphasized. For the difference between them is not one of absence and presence of ambiguity, but rather of the form and function of the ambiguities to be found in both. . . . It is common to contrast the precision of mathematics with the vagueness of poetry. But mathematics is free from vagueness only when it is purely formal, and thus lacking reference altogether. As used in science, it is descriptive, and no more precise than the terms which give it empirical reference.[24]

If we keep trying to discover the kind of ambiguity appropriate to environmental design's consequences in use, we will have created at the same time a new vocabulary for the conception of new environments. In our discussions of intention—of what we hope to do—there is much speculation about what will come to pass. Between these two terms lie the possibilities we should

24 Ernst Kris, *Psychoanalytic Explorations in Art* (New York: Schocken Books, 1964), pp. 250–251.

be trying out. It is the not trying out of possibilities that we are suffering from, and if we do not have the language for describing what we hope to do and how we do it, then we must create it. If we claim to be prevented from speculating about the possibilities because we cannot apply a presumably exact language of measurement to our hopes, then we should also recognize the barrier as the means of avoiding those failures which are always a part of trying.[25]

The importance to the creativity of the designer that I see growing out of a newly amplified design program is the same as Kris gives to the term "stringencies" below:

A problem can be constituted as such only by the existence of conditions in terms of which it is to be solved. We shall refer to these conditions in a general way as *stringencies:* they restrict the possible modes of behavior by which the problem is "legitimately" dealt with. These stringencies further differentiate the problems of aesthetic creation (and re-creation) from other sorts. In mathematics, the stringencies are maximal. . . . In the arts, stringencies . . . are minimal, . . . however, only as compared with other sorts of problem solving; in themselves they are not inconsiderable. Materials have their own properties, and the transformation of physical material to aesthetic medium requires recognition of and adaptation to these properties. . . .

Aesthetic creation is aimed at an audience: only that self-expression is aesthetic which is communicated (or communicable to others). . . . Communication lies not so much in the prior intent of the artist as in the consequent re-creation by the audience of his work of art. And re-creation is distinguished from sheer *reaction* to the work precisely by the fact that the person responding himself contributes to the stimuli for his response.[26]

25 One teacher of architecture evaluated his experimental use of what is, essentially, the kind of rich design program I have in mind. His class used a list of "human needs" ("affiliation, nurturance, security, solitude, autonomy" and so on) in thinking through the redesign of working space within a large studio: "As a source of new thoughts, questions, insights, and points of view, it both permitted us and compelled us to go beyond ordinary design considerations to think in terms of the experiential aspects of what we were making. . . . When we build something else, it will be the breadth and intensity of the project that will be worth remembering rather than the specific answers and configurations. In the next project all the specifics will be different and the way those specifics are brought together will be what matters," William Kleinsasser, "How Do You Make 'Built Homecoming'?," *AIA Journal,* December 1969, pp. 66–70. The source of the list of human needs is Peggy Peterson, "The Id and the Image: Human Needs and Design Implications," *Landmark* (student publication of the Department of Landscape Architecture, University of California, Berkeley), 1965, pp. 8–15. Another verbal illustration of how consideration of "psychological issues" can inspire and influence physical form is Christopher Alexander, "Changes in Form," *Architectural Design,* March 1970, pp. 122–125.

26 Kris, *Psychoanalytic Explorations in Art,* pp. 252 and 254.

Notice that Kris includes the active participation of the persons' own behavior as integral to the experience of the artist's intent; and that "prior intent" does not guarantee the communication of meaning itself—rather communication is dependent on the self-contribution of the recipient. In this same spirit, "proof" of the "effect" of environment on people is a search mistakenly undertaken if only the manifestations of the central nervous system are measured, without regard to people's values and purpose.

In having a greater tolerance for ambiguity, when that is the mode of knowing most appropriate, the designer would be exercising what Keats calls ˙negative capability: "when man is capable of being in uncertainties, Mysteries, doubts without any irritable reaching after fact and reason."[27] The phrase "irritable reaching" is descriptive of the outlook among designers where the underdeveloped understandings of what science is and what the social and behavioral sciences do lead to demands for "facts" and "answers" irritably made and irritably received. For the designer to be *capable* of being in uncertainties and doubts really means educating him differently than he has been and relieving him of burdens he should not be carrying. For the human scientist to be similarly capable means that he comes to distinguish between an appropriate scientism and a humane rationality.

I propose a conscious analogy with the drama.

Scene is to act as implicit is to explicit. . . . One could not deduce the detail of the action from the details of the setting, but one could deduce the quality of the act from the quality of the setting. . . . A narrow conception of scene as a motive force behind actors calls in turn for a corresponding restriction upon personality. . . . One set of scenic conditions will implement and amplify given ways and temperaments which in other situations would remain mere potentialities or unplanted seeds.[28]

The designer's "reading" of the design program begins the anal-

27 John Keats, "Letter 45. To George and Tom Keats. 21, 27 [?] December 1817," in *Criticism: Twenty Major Statements,* edited by Charles Kaplan (San Francisco: Chandler Publishing Company, undated), p. 345.

28 Kenneth Burke, *A Grammar of Motives and A Rhetoric of Motives* (New York: A Meridian Book—World Publishing Co., 1962), p. 7. Although Burke's "dramatic analogy" has not before been used in this way, to my knowledge, I have come across it in two books on housing, as a sustained metaphor. Back's *Slums, Projects, and People* uses "the terminology of the drama" to identify the interrelationships of the variables being studied. Chapter 12, "Differentiating," in *Housing Choices and Housing Constraints* employs a "social psychology of family behavior . . . specifically adapted to understanding the setting, theater, and properties employed in acting out its assigned or chosen roles in the community." (p. 306).

ogy—just as *Hamlet* is given a reading by one director different
from that given by another. Though the text, always available
for reference, is the same, it is treated with individualistic inter-
pretations, and subsequently discussed as admirable or dissatis-
fying. The text brings the creative abilities of the director and
actors to life.

Once the scenario (design program) is written, environmental
elements in support of behavior streams (acts) and behavior
circuits (scenes) can be created and explained as "stage properties": the sets are the resources for playing out the behaviors
to their fullest meanings, as delineated in the scenario. New questions can arise: What physical element can meet the behavior
to support, facilitate, or reinforce it? What extensions of the
person are essential to his purposes, such as tools, light, heat?
What behavior circuits are likely to conflict and contradict?
What different routines, collaborations, and events can use the
same resources? Which resources are preservative and affirmative? What omissions destructive?

The dramatic analogy is meant to evoke different aspects of
reality than those now being dealt with, without the prospect
of discovering a functional relationship in the statistical sense
between environment and behavior. I suppose it is simply a way
of affording greater respectability to probability as the reasonable
basis for taking action that it is. My purpose is to improve the
quality of the assertions made by designers and not to introduce
standards for scientific proof or verification; even so, the approach may yield propositions that chart new courses in interdisciplinary research. My intent is to enable the creative process
to effect a more humanly responsive environment; but because
the behavior and the resources would be specified so explicitly,
the likelihood of evaluative research once the new environment
is in use is improved.

Reusch and Kees's classic *Nonverbal Communication* demonstrates that the everyday world is a succession of clues that explain the intentions of the actors.[29] Perhaps a new way of working can arise where more "detailing"—ordinarily the precise
drawing of a construction component—is done to explain the
environmental resources intended to stand as properties cap-
turing the meanings of the scenario. (They would be a welcome

[29] Jurgen Ruesch and Weldon Kees, *Nonverbal Communication: Notes on
the Visual Perception of Human Relations* (Berkeley and Los Angeles: University of California Press, 1966).

balance to the unrevealing renderings done solely of building exteriors.) In Alexander's pattern language and the work of Brolin and Zeisel, exactly this capability is demonstrated, as they explain fully what they intend the relationship to be between the users' well-defined attributes and the particular environmental resource proposed. This discipline of giving reasons to himself will enable the designer to improve the quality of self-assertion, as he responds to the promptings of a design program with many dimensions. Not, however, that there will ever be only one interpretation of the scenario, for that is the inherent ambiguity of our entire subject. The richness of the designer's intentions is the important thing, not a "correlation."

Pater was prescient in realizing the persistent temptation of all arts toward the analogy with music. At the personal scale of human participation in the environment, behavior circuits are themes encompassing single points whose presence is essential to the whole; themes are varied and restated by permutations of the counterpoint and the harmony of the individual points. In music, the movement from point to point, in a discernible rhythm, is itself what creates the wholeness and not the "rightness" of the rules of counterpoint. The person's behavior, in the same way, unites the elements of an environment into a total meaning. Whatever rules there may be to the composition of an environment, they relate more to the attributes of each physical element's individual integrity (e.g., load-bearing capacities) and less to the realization of the unified theme.

The first criterion for 'architectural quality,' therefore, is the relevance of the different aspects. A work dominated by irrelevant aspects has no inner coherence. It may, however, *seem* satisfactory if one of the main dimensions is articulated; we are, for instance, easily deceived by a perfect but irrelevant form. The demand for relevance means that the parts of the totality ought to be interdependent. This is in accordance with the general need for order which governs all human activities and products. We should therefore stress than an *architectural* structure not only consists in an addition of articulated main dimensions, but also in the co-ordination of these dimensions. The ideal would be a structure where all components are relevant. . . . We should repeat that the relevance is a function of the totality, and not of the single dimensions. Forms and technical elements which seem . . . meaningless when seen in isolation, may find their clear justification within the totality.[30]

30 Christian Norberg-Schulz, *Intentions in Architecture* (Cambridge: M.I.T. Press, 1965), p. 181.

If once we use the drama as an analogy for explaining what objects are relevant to what behaviors, a new framework for interpretation and evaluation is opened. We might have a more intelligible vocabulary than the private jargon each new design coterie develops for explaining itself (called by a British architectural magazine, "semantic drunkenness" or "an elaborately structured defense mechanism against the dreaded cry 'the Emperor has no clothes!' ").[31] On the other side of the problem of inarticulateness, the dramatic analogy helps to overcome the problem seen by a critic of the plan for a new building for the Harvard Graduate School of Design:

Do the authors of a building program, by their inability to articulate "intangible" qualities, prejudice the outcome of such a project? They set their requirements in such a fashion as to preclude any central place for "intangible" qualities in their program, yet hedge their bets by requiring the architect to provide them nonetheless. . . . Inevitably, many sacrifices are made during the development of any project. . . . I believe we all suffer by our lack of ability to make tangible those "intangible" qualities of human association. If such qualities were given articulate and eloquent voice, we would gain common ground. . . . Further, we would not have to depend alone on the objective and quantitative criteria which form a restricted common ground at this time.[32]

But the extent to which the physical design of the environment will enable the inhabitants to fulfill their behavioral expectations in it yields always to the nonphysical aspects—the regulations, the hours of opening and closing, the maintenance and upkeep, the numbers of people using it at various times of day and season of year, and the people themselves, as they relate to each other. The social organization of the users is as much a fact as the physical organization of spaces and places. Few environments—only telephone booths perhaps—realize their scenarios within the physical constraints, and until the process of design takes that into full account during the inception process, failures in concrete are inevitable.

One way that environmental design can monitor the limitations to its independence from organizational and managerial

[31] "The painstaking development of gibberish assumed a functional guise. Something impelled me to return to *Alice Through the Looking Glass* and sure enough there it was. 'The point,' said Alice, 'is how many different things one word can mean.' 'The point,' said Humpty Dumpty, 'is *who is to be master!*' " Rupert Spade, "Semantic Drunkenness," *Architectural Design*, March 1969, p. 124.

[32] Peter Pragnell, "Some Comments on the Building [Harvard Graduate School of Design]," *Architectural Forum*, December 1969, pp. 66–67.

aspects is to include in its vocabulary of explanation those variables that *do* come under the designer's control as they have been manipulated toward the acknowledgment and facilitation of various kinds of behaviors. The lists following are only a very tentative juxtaposition to illustrate the possibility of substituting a semantic validity for the pathetic fallacy.

Properties of environmental elements the designer can affect by manipulating the variables under his control	Illustrative behaviors to be related to variables
Size (expansion/contraction)	*Contact and distance behaviors:*
Density	Getting together with others
Volume	Isolating self
Proportion	Identifying self/group
Shape	...
Order	*Work behaviors:*
Sequence	Handling large equipment/small
Adjacency	tools
Communication (face-to-face/	...
telephone)	*Nurture behaviors:*
Circulation (people/messages)	Cooking for few/many
Boundaries (sharp/indistinct)	Sleeping
Intersections	Bathing
Distance (near/far)	...
Variety-Uniformity	Walking
Exclusion-Inclusion	Riding
Distribution (close together/	Climbing stairs, ramps, escalators
dispersed)	...
Enclosure	Concentrating, learning
Linkage	Viewing message/ensemble
Continuity (connections)	Finding route
Repetition	Arriving/departing
Relations (left/right; over/under;	Waiting
before/behind)	Shopping
Information (signs/symbols)	Teaching
Direction	Self-service or being served
Sound (loud/soft)	...
Visibility	
Apertures	
Time (long-term/short-term)	
Rate (fast/slow)	
Texture (hard/soft; smooth/rough)	
Simultaneity	
Frequency	
Classification (categorizing)	
Mixture	
Permanence	

In time, we may be able to develop a taxonomy of these variables and the behaviors they relate to, just as there is now a taxonomy of materials and the aspects of building structure that they relate to. The very attempt to define the variables the designer actually deals with will improve both his own standard of research and his ability to persuade human scientists to work with him.

4
Opportunities

Introducing the very thought of human happiness itself obligates an optimistic tone. Optimism is only another kind of naïveté, say those who have abandoned it. (Why cry doom when it is right there at the corner?) But my optimism comes less from believing the best about us than from acknowledging still another limitation: we know more than we use.

If once we decide to make a useful link between environmental design and what knowledge about man there is, we might experience better places for living in, but I find that ultimately less rewarding than the reverberations from setting the process in motion and keeping it going. These are some that I see.

Basic Research in Environmental Design

Every consumer survey, sociological study, and case study reported in print raises the designer's hope that now, at last, he will find out what to do on his next project. The push for research into environment, of all kinds and at all scales, is made with the utilitarian hope of finding out what to do. But at the crunch, faced with the particulars of a site, population, budget, topography, and everything else, generalized research findings do not help the designer to find out what to do; he invents *de novo* what is to be done, meanwhile all too often inadequately responsive to his particular situation, because he does not know much about it. There are two contexts for the basic research appropriate to environmental design's organization, sources of funds, and objectives. The first is the particular context of the building, site plan, subdivision: basic research in environmental design is and has to be case-study research. The design program is not just one of many equally essential procedural steps taken along the way in the various stages of building: it is the single way in which research is done to gain behavioral and demographic data and to articulate the values and priorities of the population to use the physical environment (as a stratified sample or a consumer panel). It cannot conclude that "more research" is needed: it has to be finite, bounded, and directly useful. It has to choose particular numbers and to give reasons for doing so. Enough space, or distance, or proximity, or density is always to be answered in terms of the constraints, values, and priorities of each particular situation and population. The design program has to be a self-contained, working hypothesis about human diversity. The British term for the design program is, in fact, "the brief," a nice borrowing of a legalism that connotes that blessed state entered into in the judicial realm, where the facts of each individual case are naturally assumed to be different from any other. I have proposed earlier that federal programs take the leadership in funding the human studies during the inception phase of design; all such large-scale forces —new towns, corporations, and authorities, the larger architectural and planning offices, and major institutions—should incorporate this new way of structuring the design process. Investors' research into returns looks ahead perhaps ten or twenty years, but newly built environments stay in daily use for years countable by half-centuries. Each one deserves a far greater proportion of foresight than the building process has been defined to allow.

The second context for the basic research appropriate to environmental design is that of the enabling and limiting powers of codes, ordinances, federal and state program stipulations. Basic research should be going on continuously to question, establish, and modify the quantitative standards employed in building, housing, land development, and zoning codes as well as those in the regulations under which federal and state funds are made available. The standards can never be more than upper and lower limits, but they are often expressed as single numbers (variance and appeals procedures are supposed to cope with deviations). And so "the" standards must come to mean sets of standards obtaining under diverse conditions (of population and climate, for example) as well as for conditions of gradual improvement. Social and behavioral scientists belong in this enterprise along with the traditional complement of public health workers, engineers, planners, and architects, as much to uncover what should be studied in order to arrive at any standard as to test methods and make measurements. The evaluation of existing environments reflecting present standards, against a theory of human nature vis-à-vis the physical environment, is only the first task of a long agenda.

Of the many types of buildings and environments there are, housing stands as an example of the failure to question quantitative standards for their implications beyond the economic. The struggle in the United States in public housing has been to create a standard of living below that offered on the private market, not only in order to save money, but also in order not to overburden the poor with a livable environment. Evaluative research into multifamily rental housing, private as well as public, would find a wealth of daily adaptations made in response to undersized housing. *How much space?* has been answered

mainly by how much money there is available to spend. Whether
that matching process produces, then, *enough space*, is the next
question, and in the terms of this discussion, enough space
means to what extent the physical environment of a dwelling is
a resource for the fulfillment of the behavioral expectations
people have. A 1955 study showed that people who had moved
recently were as "dissatisfied with space as ever."[1] "What are
the dominant consumer preferences for space? In the first place,
consumers do not 'prefer' floor area, and in fact remain largely
ignorant of the amount of such space even within their current
dwellings. They 'prefer' rooms, and specify only that these be
large enough to accommodate appropriate activities and the
necessary furniture."[2] Cooper found that there was "far more
concern with the amount of *space* they have for various family
activities than . . . with the appearance of the house, either on
the inside or the outside . . . tenants seem much more concerned
about the size and arrangement of rooms in terms of convenience,
ease of maintenance, and ability to contain normal family activities, than they do in terms of privacy-needs within the
family."[3]

Parkinson's law aside, does housing tend to yield Tolstoy's experience?: "So they began living in their new home—in which,
as always happens, when they got thoroughly settled in, they
found they were just one room short."[4] The number and sizes
of rooms built into dwellings is of course a function of the desired relationship between construction and land acquisition
costs and the expected rent or sales price, and I am not addressing the complexities of housing economics and the consumer's
allocation of his dollar for other goods. But neither am I merely
thinking wishfully: the numbers and sizes of rooms allowable
under FHA mortgage insurance programs and under public

[1] Nelson N. Foote, Janet Abu-Lughod, Mary Mix Foley, Louis Winnick,
Housing Choices and Housing Constraints (New York: McGraw-Hill Book
Co., 1960), p. 228.
[2] Ibid., pp. 230–231.
[3] Clare C. Cooper, "Some Social Implications of House and Site Plan Design
at Easter Hill Village: A Case Study," Institute of Urban and Regional
Development, Center for Planning and Development Research, University of
California, Berkeley, 1965, pp. 37–38.
[4] Foote et al., *Housing Choices and Housing Constraints,* p. 224. Municipali-
ties that would use a relatively large minimum house size to restrict the
population is, of course, the dark side of this coin, and all the more reason
to mesh federal mortgage policies with basic research on conditions of
livability.

housing programs are crucial determinants of the quality of the housing stock. The money market meets these standards by lending what it costs to build them: if the minimum standards were to rise, the money would follow, although less money might go into housing and fewer units be built. But if we are building fresh a housing stock only stressful to live in, what is the good of it? Is this not environmental pollution at its most pervasive?

In 1960 *Housing Choices and Housing Constraints* found in studying the private new home market that an "extraordinary level of mechanical convenience is now accepted as a necessary part of new housing. If space is in conflict with equipment and appliances, the appliances almost always win."[5] In public housing built in Chicago between 1962 and 1965 (Robert Taylor Homes) no family—no matter what size—is permitted to use a washing machine in their apartment; there is neither space nor outlet for it, and if they own one, it must be rolled to a laundry room and brought home again; if they do not own one, the building (sixteen stories) provides none.

A report of the Douglas Commission has found that the "FHA Rehabilitation Guide for Residential Properties" permits loans to be made for rehabilitating rooms of minimum sizes "significantly below the recommended minima of many model housing codes."[6] The Kaiser Report raises the issue head-on:

The cost of housing can be reduced in two ways. The easiest way is reducing standards by using less land, providing less floor space and cutting down on quality features like insulation and appliances. A rather spacious tent, after all, can be bought for a hundred dollars. Many observers have been misled into thinking that low-cost units involve new technology; to the contrary, most often such units have been built to lower standards. The standards for subsidized housing units certainly warrant reexamination. Severely cutting standards to lower costs may be unwise. A society is judged partly by how it houses its people. A nation as wealthy as the United States need not house its poor in dwellings which fail to meet generally prevailing expectations of minimum quality.[7]

Much public housing, especially high-rise, probably should never have been built at all to such low minimum standards, on such

---

5 Ibid., p. 92.

6 Eric W. Mood, "The Development, Objective, and Adequacy of Current Housing Code Standards," in *Housing Code Standards: Three Critical Studies* (Washington, D.C.: The National Commission on Urban Problems, Research Report No. 19, 1969), p. 31.

7 The President's Committee on Urban Housing, *A Decent Home* (Washington: U.S. Government Printing Office, 1969), p. 207.

meager budgets. But the opposition would have had to have come from two sources: the architectural and planning professions, who would have needed to assess the low level of livability; and the politicians whose constituents were hoping to move in. Neither could have called upon research demonstrating the "bad effects" of *new* decent, safe, and sanitary—but undersized— housing. In 1969 the Douglas Commission said: "A critical examination of existing data upon which housing codes and standards are based will reveal that little is known about the requirements for family life. A majority of present housing code provisions are usually a combination of rule-of-thumb, personal experience, and professional judgment with limited supportive scientific data."[8]

The same observations and complaints have been made over the last forty years. In 1939, "The design of the home, in terms of the social functions for which it is supposed to provide a suitable background, is still on an altogether prescientific basis."[9] In 1944, "No specific, measurable information is available on how families live in their homes, their habits, possessions, and time-tables, their space and environmental needs, their desires and their grievances. Until the functions are known, the form can hardly be expected to follow them."[10] In 1952,

The consideration of general family types in terms of population characteristics and minimum room needs is not enough. It is necessary to analyze the activities of many and varied patterns of family life. . . . What are families' housing preferences, not in terms of physical features and gadgets, but in terms of the rela-

8 Mood, "The Development, Objective, and Adequacy of Current Housing Code Standards," p. 33.

9 Svend H. Riemer, "Family Life as the Basis for Home Planning: A Sociologist Looks at Housing Design Techniques," in *Housing For Health: Papers Presented Under the Auspices of the Committee on the Hygiene of Housing of the American Public Health Association* (Lancaster, Pa.: Science Press Printing Company, 1941), pp. 116–139 (originally presented as a paper in March 1939).

10 Jane Callaghan and Catherine Palmer, "Measuring Space and Motion," in *Family Living as the Basis for Dwelling Design, Volume 5* (New York: John B. Pierce Foundation, January 1944), p. 3. The authors report experiments in defining "space-shapes," where ordinary functions like dressing are recorded by camera and measurements made of the spatial extent of body motions. This now-defunct foundation showed great promise in defining the research task and doing a few pilot studies—now out-of-print. John Hancock Callender, "Introduction to Studies of Family Living," *Family Living as the Basis for Dwelling Design, Volume One,* December 1943; and Milton Blum and Beatrice Candee, "Family Behavior, Attitudes, and Possessions," *Family Living as the Basis for Dwelling Design, Volume Four,* January 1944.

tive importance assigned to activities competing for consideration in residential design and construction? Here is a broad field of investigation that has been neglected. To come to grips with it a breakdown of family life situations and patterns is prerequisite.[11]

In 1962, evaluating postwar housing in Great Britain, "the houses . . . were sometimes felt to demand too much of their owners. Their lightness and clarity seemed to forbid human failings; the flotsam and jetsam of family life were out of place; every cat had to be a Siamese."[12]

The problem of defining acceptable measures of housing deficiency is still being wrestled with by both industrial and developing societies.[13] But it is not the building that we should be measuring as "sound, deteriorating, or dilapidated" but instead the people in it, as they bear the costs of adaptation to incongruent environments. The standard used for determining "crowding" in the United States census relates to the numbers of persons per room, and when there are more than 1.01 persons per room, a dwelling is defined as overcrowded. Room sizes do not enter into the measure. The crowding of households has customarily referred to doubled-up families riding out a housing or income shortage and to the stuffing of families into single rooms by slum landlords. We refer to "high density" housing, where the ratio of total floor area to land area is tight, but this is a measure implying a relation between occupants and the "open space" available at the site. When one person can be "crowded" in a "room" of Lilliputian dimensions, we should admit to having no perspective on the livability of housing.

An exercise by students dramatized the disparity between what we know and what we use. They first defined as many behavior circuits as they could think might occur in the ordinary lives of a family of six, with two girls aged 7 and 12 and two boys, 3 and 16. The exercise postulated that each child has a hobby and friends; that the mother sews the family clothes; that the father is active in the PTA and local politics; that the family occupies a three-bedroom apartment. (The exercise did not allow for the

11 Svend Riemer and Nicholas J. Demerath, "The Role of Social Research in Housing Design," *Land Economics*, Vol. 28, No. 3, August 1952, p. 232.
12 Elisabeth Beazley, *Designed to Live In* (London: Allen & Unwin, 1962), p. 109.
13 For example, Anatole A. Solow, "Some Reflections on 'Realistic' Minimum Standards in Housing," paper prepared for the First International Conference on Health Research in Housing and Its Environment, Pittsburgh, Pa., February 1970, 31 pp. mimeo.

family's values and priorities, which could lead it to value other things more than a house of adequate size.) After identifying the behavior circuits, the students named and measured the resources needed for carrying them out by using standard, published data giving human dimensions standing, walking, sitting, reaching, as well as furniture sizes and clearances needed for vacuuming and bedmaking.[14] The dimensioned behavior circuits were juxtaposed on the architectural plan for an existing three-bedroom apartment in public housing. Even when furniture was rearranged and allowances made for the sequential use of space instead of simultaneous use, the public housing provided only a partial resource for family living. The most minimal approach illustrated that the dwelling provided only 60 percent of the space needed for carrying out ordinary family pursuits; a generous, but hardly unrealistic, approach calculated that the dwelling unit provided merely 5 percent of the floor area needed to accommodate the human and nonhuman resources family members need.[15]

New Pleadings in the Law

The main social issue that these ideas may affect over the longest run is the more equitable allocation of public resources among groups. The meaning to the lives of people of the disparities in the distribution of public resources has not been established much beyond ideology. Some ideologies become law with little

[14] Helen E. McCullough, Kathryn Philson, Ruth H. Smith, Anna L. Wood, and Avis Woolrich, *Space Standards for Household Activities*, Bulletin 686, University of Illinois Agricultural Experiment Station, May 1962; "Chapter III. Basic Functional Space Needs," in *Planning the Home for Occupancy* (Chicago: Public Administration Service, 1950), pp. 17–36; Francis deN. Schroeder, *Anatomy for Interior Designers* (New York: Whitney Publications, 1948).

[15] The Department of Housing and Urban Development will be replacing its room-size standards for both public and private housing with "Unit Design Criteria" in which no minimum room sizes are specified, but instead requirements are stated for "appropriate space" to be designed in terms of rooms having *furnishings* of specified minimum amounts and sizes with specified "minimum clearances" around them. Whether these amounts and sizes of furniture will become not the minimum, but as always, the standard, will depend on the spirit and concepts guiding their administration. Permission is given to include an extra room (den or bedroom) in apartments. The industrialized housing proposals coming out of "Operation Breakthrough" are the first to use these new criteria, which have been published as "Operation Breakthrough" RFP-Attachment, I (RFP H-55-69), pp. 1–37, Department of Housing and Urban Development, Washington, D.C. A report of a prototype of low-cost housing "breaking out from the limitations of minimal planning" at the Cambridge University School of Architecture (England) is reported in John Hix, "Maximum House Space," *Architectural Design*, March 1970, pp. 148–149.

argument because the cultural climate allows it. Though we had the ideology about equal educational opportunity for a long time, it was not until the social sciences provided data on learning differentials that the ideology became persuasive to the Supreme Court. The current federal effort at "social indicators"[16] is ultimately pointed toward persuasion, but until the categories in which data are now conceived and collected are changed, the capability for measurement is limited.[17]

What is measured makes the crucial difference. If the concepts I have suggested were put to use widely, it is very likely that new interest groups in society would be uncovered. In defining the ingredients of "social systems accounting," Gross sees the same likelihood when "subjective" interests, as opposed to the more readily quantifiable "objective" interests of groups in society, are taken into statistical consideration. To define what he sees as constituting "subjective interests"—but without naming the data that would substantiate them—Gross has made a synthesis of the motivation theories of Maslow, Horney, Murray, Goldstein, Fromm, and Selye, arriving at three concepts: belonging, participation, affection; status, respect, power; and self-fulfillment, beauty, creativity. He says that the discussion of subjective interests "tends to degenerate into the empty phrases and glittering generalities of propagandistic perorations."[18] But perhaps that can change as human studies in the inception phase begin to be made that tell us more specifically what it is about people their human and nonhuman environment relates to, with what consequences, with what intensities of importance to them. The respectably quantitative context of environmental "assets and deficits" can record aspiration and failure.

Right now we could do with a new way of conceiving the qualitative disparities between the assets of the suburbs in which

16 U.S. Department of Health, Education, and Welfare, *Toward A Social Report* (Washington, D.C.: U.S. Government Printing Office, 1969).

17 In trying to match the explicit statements of specific goals in the report of the President's Commission on National Goals of 1960 with readily available statistical indicators, and using very loose criteria of relevance, Biderman found that "for only 59 per cent of the goal statements are any indicator data in these sources judged pertinent"—moreover, the least numbers of indicators were found for "arts and sciences" and "technological change." Albert D. Biderman, "Social Indicators and Goals," in *Social Indicators*, edited by Raymond A. Bauer (Cambridge: M.I.T. Press, 1966), pp. 87–88.

18 Bertram M. Gross, *The State of the Nation: Social Systems Accounting* (London: Social Science Paperbacks, Tavistock Publications, 1966), pp. 89 and 100.

city dwellers do not share and the deficits—air pollution, bad housing, traffic congestion—of the cities in which suburbanites do not share (or do not share fully—as yet). For example, regional open space in metropolitan areas that is supposed to serve the entire population is usually located in the suburban areas and it is not functionally accessible to lower income populations without cars. What is the meaning of "regional open space" in the lives of people? What behavioral expectations do people in the inner city have that are disappointed by the inaccessibility of the countryside? What consequences does this have in the behavioral adaptations they make in the absence of environmental resources to meet these expectations? What are the observable individual and social costs within each of the essential striving sentiments? The ultimate remedy for functional inaccessibility may be quite simple—free bus service or subsidized car rental—but the establishment of public policy, in statute and budget, will require evidence for justifying the inclusion of new human values in the law. Similar questions remain unasked about housing, schools, health services—those issues with which designers and planners are dealing in their own ways and human scientists in still others. In the breach between is public discontent and unrest on the one hand and, on the other, repeatedly misguided public policy. But we are told in 1969 by a committee of the National Academy of Sciences that to "develop the major social and behavioral science research efforts needed by the nation's cities and by the Department of Housing and Urban Development will take at least five years under favorable conditions."[19] The most prestigious and powerful members of academic social and behavioral science could help to create one "favorable condition" if they would begin to value and reward teaching and research reaching beyond what the same report calls "disciplinary separatism and myopia."[20]

Besides finding new groups whose interests are made measurable, a new context is taking hold for judging detriments to the public well-being. Nader, working strictly within the legal system, has opened new channels for making moral criteria operational.[21]

19 Report of the Committee on Social and Behavioral Urban Research, *A Strategic Approach to Urban Research and Development: Social and Behavioral Science Considerations* (Washington, D.C.: Division of Behavioral Science, National Research Council, National Academy of Sciences, 1969), p. 2.
20 Ibid., p. 53.
21 Marti Mueller, "Nader: From Auto Safety to a Permanent Crusade," *Science*, 21 November 1969, pp. 979–983.

Common urban complaints—air pollution, overcrowded buses, bad housing—also belong in a new context of *human* degradation —not, as the phrase has it, environmental degradation. When the environmental resources people require do not exist at all or exist unreliably, then society is saying "your purposes are unimportant"—when those purposes may be to get a job outside of the ghetto, to go to school regularly, to keep up friendships. For Americans, housepride is another way of expressing self-esteem: society is saying "self-esteem is unimportant" when it fails to build housing, to clean streets, to plant trees, to modernize garbage disposal methods.

"Emerson said that life was not worth having just for doing tricks in; and technics is not just a way of running to and fro and seeking out many inventions: it is a means of creating a human personality more capable of meeting the forces of nature on even terms and more capable of directing rationally its own life."[22] Our humanness is sustained in very great measure by complex machinery, invented and run by men. It is when the machinery fails to work or spews disease that we are diminished and our relatedness falls into disjunction. Urban mechanics, then, can be regarded as a creative extension of ourselves, all the more to be raged at when it moves against our purposes or fail to move at all when we need it. Our transit systems, power supply, oxygen, driving channels are nonhuman analogues for completely human purposes. If we concentrate merely on their existence as objects, then we dehumanize their meaning because we are the only source of it. As Nader is doing with consumer products, so might we name and reject the negative meanings to our lives of these technologies that have promised much and delivered little, badly.

A Wider Vocabulary in Use

A Reorientation of Community Studies. Ten years ago Maurice Stein published *The Eclipse of Community,* an appraisal of those few enduring studies in American sociology that have yielded a rich understanding of some basic social processes.[23] Stein labors little over the question of the relationship between environment and social organization,[24] because his main concern is to show

22 Lewis Mumford, *Art and Technics* (New York: Columbia University Press, 1952), p. 55.
23 Maurice R. Stein, *The Eclipse of Community: An Interpretation of American Studies* (New York: Harper Torchbooks, 1964), published originally in 1960 by the Princeton University Press.
24 Ibid., p. 112.

how the sociologist can avoid being so much identified with the mass society he studies as to use research methods which reinforce depersonalization, deindividuation, alienation: "No matter how tremendous the pressure to treat oneself and others as objects in mass society, vital human dramas are still enacted. . . . It is the special responsibility of the community study to keep these dramas continually in focus. No matter how far from the center of the stage, they do provide a meeting ground for people within a community which the depersonalizing forces of mass society can diminish but never destroy. There is even a possibility that sociologists will contribute to the enlargement of these meeting grounds, but this can happen only if we keep reminding ourselves that we are studying *human* communities and if we mold our theories and methods accordingly."[25] He points out that what the sociologist can gain from an anthropological perspective is the organizing idea of the celebration of major life transitions: "the image of primitive society supplied us by Radin, Redfield, and Sapir, in which integral human functioning through an intelligible life cycle where major human needs are assured of satisfaction and major life transitions directly confronted, helps us to formulate norms for human community life."[26] And he suggests that what the psychoanalytic perspective reveals are those "developmental tasks . . . necessary for helping human beings to reach full community participation."[27] Finally, Stein frames the role of the dramatic analogy in sociology: "the central problem of the community sociologist is to achieve an objective perspective that encompasses the partial perspectives held by various groups in the community in such a fashion as to call attention to hidden processes without losing sight of the meaning of the various partial perspectives."[28]

The parallels abound between the concerns of his work and this one, as well they might. I read Stein ten years ago and simply trusted that such a profound and sensible redirection would overtake the study of community life in cities and suburbs, whether by sociologists or city planners. Stein's future work will tell us whether a change has taken hold in his field, but this book represents the cumulative realization that it has not in mine. Lamentably, the "vital human dramas" of environmental de-

25 Ibid., p. 303.
26 Ibid., p. 248.
27 Ibid., p. 268.
28 Ibid., p. 325.

sign in the past decade have been enacted mainly in public hearings and courtrooms, where people protest the sacrifice of home and neighborhood to housing they cannot afford or highways they never use. Political science has made an abundant case-history literature out of urban and metropolitan decision-making processes. But the concepts used to formulate research on environmental issues have not been so changed or responsive; the 1970 census data categories will not reflect any conceptual innovations. Stein's research prospectus is still largely unfulfilled by city and regional planning:

A far more complete picture of the levels of participation in and response to mass society must be obtained. This is a prerequisite for reformulation of Park's theory of natural areas. No amount of theorizing can identify the range of urban sub-communities in the modern city, nor can it describe their structures or their interrelations. Ecological and demographic data help to provide starting points for explorations into metropolitan social structures. Park's injunction to "get out and look" bears repeating. The single category "suburbia" contains at least three sub-types as exemplified by Park Forest, Crestwood Heights, and exurbia. There is good reason to suppose that many others will be found. Our cities obviously contain working-class suburbs, occupational communities, new kinds of business districts like the huge peripheral shopping centers, and even Bohemias.[29]

A redirection of community studies would offer, for example, the identification of emerging forms of social organization whose need for physical manifestation can be evaluated. Uncovering the meanings of small-scale and particular "institutions"—arrangements people make for dealing with recurrent problems of everyday living—would help the designer to respond with ideas for physical resources distributed where they will be used. For example, the supermarket shopping cart that also holds a child may be one such "institution" that reveals much about kinship arrangements or child care facilities or the availability of daytime babysitters in the neighborhood. Or the seemingly increasing use of streets and sidewalks by teenagers and unemployed men may have functions for these groups unrecognized by traditional settlement houses or recreation spaces.

29 Ibid., p. 301. Chapin, writing in 1965 in *Urban Land Use Planning*, implies such work remains a future task: "Participant-observer studies of anthropologists and sociologists are helping to supply the planning field with a fuller appreciation of modes of human behavior of significance in land use planning. They involve a specialized form of investigation which shows promise of adaptation to city planning needs and becoming a part of the continuing survey and study effort of planning agencies . . ." p. 38.

Carry-out shops, laundromats, and records shops have recently come to the ghetto in numbers. They join taverns, pool halls, liquor stores, corner groceries, rooming houses, secondhand stores, credit houses, pawnshops, industrial insurance companies, and storefront churches as parts of a distinctive complex of urban institutions that have undergone changes in adapting to the effective wants, limited choices, and mixed tastes of inner-city residents. Inner-city carry-out shops serve many functions other than selling prepared food. Among other things they may serve as informal communication centers, forums, places to display and assess talents, and staging areas for a wide range of activities, legal, illegal, and extralegal. And although they exist in the heart of the city, they are like outpost institutions—gathering places for outsiders in the center of the city.[30]

Morris has pointed out the existence of a new group he likens to the European immigrant in testing this society's commitment to pluralism: "If we put these four groups together—the young and the old, the disabled, the poor, and the addicted or mentally ill—we have a new kind of minority, a deviant mass of persons, deviant in the sense that they do not conform to the medical or social ideas of the healthy, vigorous person capable of managing his affairs the way the rest of us manage ours. . . . The significant fact is that these groups lack the mobility which the trends in our society seem to require." Morris suggests that city neighborhoods might develop that permit addicts, for example, to live in "tolerant acceptance," where health and social facilities would be located too. Instead of sending the sick off to institutions, he suggests they be cared for at home, so the sick and the well live together under a panoply of "special schools, half-way houses, day care centers, home health and nursing services," using the decentralization of such services as a means of city-building.[31]

Gans has recommended, for example, to the developers of Columbia that if second generation ethnic groups are to be expected to buy houses and move there from Baltimore and Philadelphia, that arrangements be made to permit the women to telephone toll-free to their mothers as an especially useful device for luring them out of their close-knit locales.[32] Besides

[30] Hylan Lewis, "Foreword," in Elliot Liebow, *Tally's Corner: A Study of Negro Streetcorner Men* (Boston: Little, Brown and Company, 1967), pp. vii–viii. See also Ulf Hannerz, *Soulside: Inquiries into Ghetto Culture and Community* (New York: Columbia University Press, 1969) and Gerald Suttles, *The Social Order of the Slum* (Chicago: University of Chicago Press, 1969).
[31] Robert Morris, "The City of the Future and Planning for Health," *American Journal of Public Health*, Vol. 58, No. 1, January 1968, pp. 17 and 20.
[32] Herbert J. Gans, "Planning for the Everyday Life and Problems of Sub-

making the latent manifest, community studies could also describe and compare various interactive and socializing processes in sufficient depth that substitutes for them might become viable alternatives in public policy (jitney buses, subsidized bicycles for children).

The same committee of the National Academy of Sciences is looking for ways of measuring the "quality of life," and what remains still to be found out about community reflects our lack of a theory of human nature for environmental design.

Considerable folk knowledge exists about "good" neighborhoods, but little systematic research has been done either on them or on the conception of a "good" neighborhood. . . . If the neighborhood as a system can be shown to bear an important causal relation to the functioning of schools, of normative structures, of control systems and deviance, of sense of competence and ability to affect one's own fate, of the maintenance of social and personal capital, of capacity for cooperative action, and of other matters of critical importance, then research should be aimed at providing the best empirical and theoretical understanding of neighborhood that current research capabilities permit. . . . The development of a theoretical understanding of neighborhood functioning requires observation of a variety of neighborhoods and a conceptualization of observations and measurements that will permit making significant comparisons and the editing of theory.[33]

Responses to Aggression and Sex. As the analysis in the appendix illustrates, what environmental designers have seen as satisfying to "human needs" cluster around the sentiments relative to status, identity, and group belonging. The clusters of sentiments represented in Leighton's terminology of sexual satisfaction, of expressing and securing love, and of expressing hostility, though they are made manifest in human behaviors, do not find their way so readily into either designers' thought processes or into the physical analogues of the environment. Mumford has been, of course, an incomparable commentator on the gracious aspects of sex and love in Central Park; Jane Jacobs has been, of course, an incomparable detractor of New York's parks, claiming that nothing gentle is likely to go on in them. Jacobs and Mumford are addressing two human attributes whose urban expressions seem increasingly discomforting, sex and aggression.

urban and New Town Residents," in *People and Plans: Essays on Urban Problems and Solutions* (New York: Basic Books, 1968), p. 193.
33 Report of the Committee on Social and Behavioral Urban Research, *A Strategic Approach*, p. 30.

The period of late adolescence, when sexual energies run high and direct outlets are relatively few, is a trying and difficult one for both boys and girls. Often it is a period of inner disruption, whose very turmoil should be counterbalanced by the wonder and beauty of the environment. If prolongation of infancy was the first mark of Man's ascent, the prolongation of courtship, with all its rich by-products in art, literature, music, and religion, represents a further stage. This elaboration of the erotic impulse also intensified it, adding meaning and emotional color to purely instinctual manifestations. In the open country, lovers have little difficulty in finding places of seclusion that match their mood, but the lack of such walks and retreats in our cities, even in our parks, makes courtship too often either brief or furtive, harassed or embarrassed to the point of desperation. . . .

What lovers need are accessible places where they can easily lose themselves and get away from the visible presence of others. The maze, that favorite device of Baroque planners, certainly served that purpose; and Frederick Law Olmsted, in designing Central Park in New York, deliberately made The Ramble, with its irregular topography, a place to get lost in; with the admirable result that it is perhaps the one place well adapted to lovemaking in the whole city of New York. If planners were conscious of the phases of life, they would not be so blank about the need of late adolescence for places of secluded beauty, accentuating and expanding, and yet tempering, their erotic needs; and enriching, with happy visual images, their erotic rewards.[34]

The changing sexual and familial lives of both lower income Negro populations and divorced white middle- and upper-class professionals may soon require new kinds of recognition in public policy. The changes in women's roles and the growing populations of women with children but no husband—whether never married, divorced, separated, or widowed—are going to require eventual recognition in new societal institutions and new kinds of environments for them to live in. As more mothers take jobs, the child care arrangements handled in the past by extended family systems are becoming a widespread matter of public interest. Women are newly interested in adult education and self-improvement facilities, conveniently located. The planning of any new and large-scale project, whether or not public, is the logical place to raise various questions that these cultural changes prompt: What kind of dwelling does the unmarried mother need different from the dwelling of a traditional family unit? What day care facilities for preschool children can be provided in a new subdivision as well as in a high-rise building? Can com-

[34] Lewis Mumford, "Planning for the Phases of Life" (1949), *The Urban Prospect* (London: Secker & Warburg, 1968), pp. 31–32.

munal food preparation and eating arrangements be accommodated? What adult education and training facilities are within range by foot, by bus, by car?

The problems of aggression in the city, short of rioting and guerilla warfare, are clear in Mrs. Coit's identification of "environmental difficulties" in high-rise public housing and they are clear in the fabric of life in many American cities today. As one emotional consequence of low income, unemployability, and unemployment, experienced by so many blacks—and the threats felt by working-class whites—human aggression has little to do directly with environmental design. But aggression as a human fact might be acknowledged in the human use of housing, neighborhoods, public buildings, transit systems. The environment already deals with the likelihood of some kinds of aggressive, hostile, and destructive behaviors: fences, locks, high walls, durable materials, policemen, alarm boxes, public telephones. The way that the environment enters into people's expressions of aggression and hostility, usually interpersonal in origin, is often as an object of them, either for itself or as a displacement of feelings away from others onto the inanimate. What might the physical response be if the fact of these behaviors were taken into account positively as well as defensively and protectively? Aggression is often born of frustration—of the blocking of other behavior—so that resources for fulfilled behaviors are essential for reducing its intensity. Can we also seek a realistic distinction between aggression as a purposeful public menace and aggression as inherent in the ordinary processes of meeting life's conflicts and stresses?

No matter what the possible answers may turn out to be, I mean only to emphasize that new low-income housing designed without reference to the hostile and aggressive behaviors of its inhabitants to each other and to their environment will be unsatisfactory to live in and to manage; just as planning for new suburban subdivisions that fails to take these same aspects of human behavior into account is bound to bear similar consequences.

In cities and suburbs, the two constellations of sex and aggression unite at high pitch in adolescents. "Juvenile delinquency" occurs everywhere, but in the suburbs especially the entire question of teenagers' behavioral expectations and the lack of resources with which to meet them is an issue yet to be faced by public policy. There, unacceptable as they may be to the adults, they have few routes of flight, and the arguments over using and paying for the family car form a kind of lightning rod for the ordinary stresses of this phase of family life. The proponents of highways and the detractors of public transit systems to serve the suburbs are, quite directly, fostering a generation of disaffected adults.

Tinbergen has hesitantly concluded after reviewing the Lorenz and Morris work on aggression in animals and man that because the urge to fight is innate, whatever the cause, we must find "ways and means for keeping our intergroup aggression in check." He recommends redirection or sublimation—in the form of "a scientific attack on our own behavioral problems."[35] Questions about troubling urban and suburban problems will not be raised unless the constellation of aggressive, hostile, and avoidance behaviors is acknowledged as natural to the condition of the human use of the physical environment beyond the punitive and repressive ways used now. A reconceptualization of recreation—such a green and promising land-use category—to acknowledge human strivings to express aggression and hostility might create different physical forms in high density urban settings. Again, this is not to be understood as suggesting a correlation or direct effect; only that when outdoor recreation facilities are being planned to accommodate various populations in various settings, behaviors expressing aggression and hostility are likely to occur and need recognition ahead of time. Land use arrangements that exacerbate likely conflicts between people can be said to add to the general level of tensions and mobilization of bad feeling. One arrangement most often destructive in these very terms is the location of play space vis-à-vis housing: children of all ages are noisy at play; the noise they make is often a concomitance of competitive and aggressive behavior; the reaction from annoyed adults can be equally noisy and aggressive. Physical separation is not always possible—what acoustic protections might be installed over or around the outdoor space? In itself, this would be a new environmental response to a newly uncovered human requirement. Lynch has proposed a new context for rethinking urban recreation space, leading also to new environmental responses for newly acknowledged human purposes:

For his satisfaction and growth an individual needs opportunities to engage in active interchange with his environment: to

35 N. Tinbergen, "On War and Peace in Animals and Man," *Science*, 28 June 1968, p. 1418.

use it, change it, organize it, even destroy it. His physical surroundings should be accessible and open-ended, challenging, wayward, responsive to effort. . . . Open space is more easily accepted as being of public concern than is the planning of city centers, but our range of ideas in dealing with this feature is extremely narrow. Public open space usually means an athletic field, a beach, a lawn with trees and shrubs, a woodland, with trails and picnic areas, perhaps a central plaza. Many other kinds can easily be imagined: mazes, heaths, thickets, canyons, rooftops, caves, marshes, canals, undersea gardens, yards for certain hobbies. We should design for diversity, experiment with new types, open recreational choices, fit opportunities to the real diversity of city people and their values.[36]

The Suburban Skeleton. One recurrent theme stressed in naming the plights of our world is the loss of personal identity and consequently the loss of a sense of community, or vice versa. Though it is possible to conclude that the quality of civilization is diminished if people withdraw their moral energies from the larger group and if our participatory democracy relies on an ever-decreasing elite, that does not mean we should not also make the attempt to find out what people are doing instead. If we do, perhaps we can then create the resources they need for those pursuits, which are also human pursuits, so that they can find reflected in the world about them a recognition of themselves. Some activities may be more valuable to people's lives than they give the appearance of being, especially to urban romanticists. The people who used to sit colorfully on stoops in tenement districts, giving visible evidence of a "cohesive" community, are living now in "upwardly mobile" suburbs, doing different things: perhaps they are more private and more self-determined.

"Sense of community" is often seen revolving around response to personal crisis, when people in the vicinity can be mobilized to help. At the time of a crisis it is far more likely for help to be readily forthcoming, but the everyday round is where loneliness and alienation are defined. And so what kind, what quality of, contact do we really mean when we speak of physical layouts that may maximize the opportunities people have for interacting? Visual contact, the ritual of polite response to greetings, and the occasional favor are indeed a kind of neighborly contact that should be customary; when it is gone from a neighborhood,

[36] Kevin Lynch, "The City As Environment," in *Cities: A 'Scientific American' Book* (London: Penguin Books, 1967), pp. 205 and 207.

as it can be in the ghetto, on account of mutual suspicions, for example, then there may be social pathology. But if we assume that people quite naturally make such customary contact with each other, and that it is of a superficial kind, and that we are interested in a society where people are enabled to invest their moral energies in the larger community—then does it not seem quite off the target to have concentrated on only a few pat stereotypes of "community focal points," usually shopping areas, to provide a sense of community and a sense of belonging? It is not that handsome shopping areas and plazas are unjustifiable in human terms; they can make the everyday necessity of shopping a positive pleasure. Community halls and swimming pools are basic assets too. But what other environmental analogues might there be for behaviors that express substantive involvement, identity with a larger group, and belonging? A large public garden for anyone to work in, as a substitute for individual and costly lawn-tending; or cooperative stockholding in a small movie house or a local jitney service are examples of new forms of semipublic organizations and facilities that may enhance the sense of community.[37]

So frequently do suburban subdivisions lack the physical analogues for ordinary life that they are merely orderly skeletons, two-dimensional representations of two-dimensional paper plans. All those very small scale activities that splice cities together into manageable circuits for people on their daily round can and should belong in the suburbs we already have. Their "monotony" and "dullness"—either visually or socially—can be read as stating what has been left out: the resources not there to meet behavioral expectations that are. We should begin to assume that we can flesh out these bare bones whenever we want to; it requires only sufficient wit and imagination to overturn local zoning prohibitions on corner stores, cobblers, garages, home industries, high density housing for elderly parents. Acoustic and landscaping screens, for helping to make disparate uses

[37] "In the study of gardening in two Chicago suburbs conducted by our Center for the Study of Leisure . . . we found in Fairlawn, a new developer's suburb . . . that to many housewives the garden was simply one more chore. It represented neither a contrast with the asphalt jungle of the city, nor a pleasure in growing things, nor a rage for order. It was rather a tax imposed by neighborhood consciousness—the neighbors often being interpreted as more concerned and censorious than they, for the most part, were." David Riesman, "The Suburban Dislocation," *The Annals of the American Academy of Political and Social Science,* Vol. 314, November 1957, p. 139.

compatible in scale and atmosphere, are certainly within the realm of possibility. But before any such changes, perhaps new forms of property insurance might be devised to protect home-owners from loss once these different uses and especially higher density housing, the favorite shibboleth of real estate mythology, are introduced.[38]

Abrams has foreseen the suburbs as "the next generation's main encampment," but needing to be better than they are:

Suburban development programs however, have demonstrated little capacity for dealing with the human aspects of community life, and programs like FHA have found little room in their manuals for such commonplace things as meeting and mating, or walking and browsing, or giving people a sense of belonging, or adding something of ourselves to the prepackaged community, or expanding the opportunities for adult education, or providing escape hatches from the sameness of living.[39]

The stock of prototypes in housing grows constantly. The picture book industry flourishes, and the latest projects are copied around the world. Standards in federal, state, and local regulations enforce prototypes too. What, then, of human diversity and a diversity of environmental responses? In its fullest definition, a theory of human nature for environmental design includes as well the striving for equality of opportunity for each person to choose freely where he wants to live, what proportion of income he spends for housing, the neighbors and schools he wants. Doing battle with the constraints on such freedom—race prejudice, low income, inadequate education, unemployability, zoning restrictions, unnecessary construction costs, high interest rates—is thus as integral a function of environmental design as drawing plans: In order to have diversity the designer must be free to formulate a unique reading of a scenario, as a working hypothesis to be carried out in brick and mortar. To be free, he must know that what he has left out and not emphasized will be taken up by still other designers' readings. The consumer must be free as well to choose among these many possibilities. A

[38] "Is there a need to ensure that low income units do not erode the value and equity of medium-income living space? Should there be a counterpart of the Federal Deposit Insurance mechanism?" in a report by the Committee on Urban Technology, *Long-Range Planning for Urban Research and Development: Technological Considerations* (Washington, D.C.: Division of Engineering, National Research Council, National Academy of Science, 1969), p. 40.

[39] Charles Abrams, "Housing in the Year 2000," in *Environment and Policy: The Next Fifty Years,* William R. Ewald, Jr., editor (Bloomington: Indiana University Press, 1968), p. 216.

diversity of housing types juxtaposed in a single neighborhood is sure to be a consequence of the court tests of exclusionary zoning in the suburbs and of court decisions that public housing has to be built in white neighborhoods too. The quality and livability of the physical design is one that can preserve and affirm goodwill and harmony, as important an opportunity as any for changing in its fundamentals the theory and practice of environmental design.

What Will a Responsive Environment Look Like?

A more responsive and humane environment will very likely look different from current aesthetic ideals at each end of the range, such as they are: neither steely glass boxes set in an Elysian field of tidy typography nor whitewashed villages for strollers in perpetual sunshine. The significance of the coming environment will be in its smaller scale, its variety, and its flexibility.

In both city and suburb the form of locomotion will better suit the trip, with choice among bikes, jitneys, and minibuses. Much single-family housing is likely to stay strictly conventional, straitlaced, and look-alike, to please what the continuously new middle class sees as "having arrived." The insides of apartment houses—whether or not reflected on the outside—will hold many activities usually separate: corner stores, child care centers, cafeterias, community rooms. Half-finished or "shell" housing will help lower-income families to ownership, and this principle of open-endedness will be extended to the larger scale of "new towns," where decisions will be left unmade on purpose, to learn after the residents have settled in just what they expect in their daily round—whether more recreation areas or parking or gardens. Traditional buildings will carry dual roles, as churches are used for weekday nursery schools, elementary schools for adult education, restaurants as the meeting places of different age groups. Fewer great spaces will appear as such; they will be broken up around the city into smaller places for informal things to happen in—jogging, gardening, strumming, talking. Play spaces will range from the unimaginative, as now, to messy adventure; but they will be likely to sprout between boxy, cold buildings.

The setting people will be most involved in is *home*—inside. Everyone will be at home, to see color television, listen to records, visit with friends from all over, carry on hobbies of collecting and making. People without much money are the likeliest to stay home. Whether home is a setting for really growing up in depends very much on many things going on well beyond it. But as a setting for what goes on there that cannot go on anywhere else, it is a precious resource.

Taken in all, diversity, if taken seriously, can ultimately mean that the traditional class and status distinctions preserved by zoning and building regulations become the overt public issues they deserve to be, and more meaningful criteria are used to combine and separate land uses. And so the unity of the landscape will be far more in the beholder and less in the forms, partly by his freer use of different kinds of places and partly by his seeing so much more about himself he is familiar with. The coming environment will reassure us that we can enter it and respond, because it reflects things we know about ourselves.

Appendix

The analysis here represents a very rough measurement of the scope of the current vocabulary the designer works with at the drawing board in thinking about people—what designers think is important to have in mind as they go about creating a physical environment. I have classified two lists of environmental attributes and resources compiled by persons trained in architecture and city planning in terms of Leighton's concepts, stretching the attributes' significance into a relationship with his elaborated definitions of the "essential striving sentiments." Each item so classified represents something that the designer has thought about, regardless of its validity. Both of the original lists were written, however, by designers who represent aware and conscientious work in their field, and they have not been selected for this analysis with the prior bias that they would necessarily display a narrow vocabulary. By their very explicitness in compiling such specific statements, they are already searching for a wider grasp of human nature.

An "Amenity Attributes" list was compiled for the San Francisco Community Renewal Program for a study of the "Amenity Attributes of Residential Locations."[1] Another list, of "Site Planning Elements," was compiled for their own use in designing a residential area by graduate students in the Urban Design Program of the Department of City and Regional Planning, University of Pennsylvania in 1966.

Interestingly, the "Amenity Attributes" are couched mainly in negative terms—that in order to have amenity in a neighborhood, the attribute should not be there. The syntax emphasizes the point made in this book: that if we can learn to concentrate on the fulfillment of behavioral expectations in the environmental resources we create, we may be more likely to discover genuine innovations at the drawing board. The main point of an analysis such as this is simply to ask, given an expanded vocabulary of what is human, what ideas might designers come up with? Readers are encouraged to make their own, equally subjective, classification of these lists.

[1] Sim van der Ryn, "Amenity Attributes of Residential Locations," Technical Paper No. 3, 1966, with methods developed by Christopher Alexander, San Francisco Community Renewal Program, pp. A-1–A-8.

List 1. Attributes that should not be present in order for a neighborhood to have amenity

PHYSICAL SECURITY
Parents do not have a sense children are safe
Lack of visual privacy
Streets and sidewalks in poor condition

SEXUAL SATISFACTION
None

THE EXPRESSION OF HOSTILITY
None

THE EXPRESSION OF LOVE
Parents do not have a sense children are safe
Poor neighborly cohesion

THE SECURING OF LOVE
Poor neighborly cohesion

THE EXPRESSION OF SPONTANEITY
No socially acceptable provision for active group recreation nearby
Unsatisfactory public transport
Difficult to achieve personal anonymity
Little variety of street life
Unsatisfactory time-distance to nearest food store

THE SECURING OF RECOGNITION
Poor neighborly cohesion
No "gracious living"
No provision for decency and respectability in the form of the suburban image

ORIENTATION IN TERMS OF ONE'S PLACE IN SOCIETY AND THE PLACES OF OTHERS
Outdoor space poorly maintained
Low-income, low-class people
Dwelling: poor transition from street to house
The area has no name which represents status to given groups
Poor neighborly cohesion
No physical enclave, no feeling of enclosure or "wholeness"
Lack of picturesque character
No feeling that street and sidewalk belong to you
No opportunity to satisfy the desire for property ownership: "a home of your own"
No distinctive identity to dwelling unit or building
Area is uninviting to pedestrian use both day and night

Nonhomogeneous social environment

Lack of visual privacy

No historic character: no opportunity to express desire for continuity of local tradition and life style

No provision of personal services

Lack of interior privacy

No used or usable private outdoor space

THE SECURING AND MAINTAINING OF MEMBERSHIP IN A DEFINITE HUMAN GROUP

No opportunity to display income status through external appearance of residence

Constraint of bourgeois milieu

Lack of opportunity to express difference of life style in external appearance of dwelling

The area has no name which represents status to given groups

Poor quality public school

No feeling that street and sidewalk belong to you

Little variety of street life

No opportunity to satisfy the desire for property ownership: "a home of your own"

No distinctive identity to dwelling unit or building

No provision for decency and respectability in the form of the suburban image

No community center or community accepted indoor neighborhood gathering place, including recreational facilities

No historic character: no opportunity to express desire for continuity of local tradition and life style

Deserted daytime streets, lack of street life

Presence of residents that prevailing user types are prejudiced against

No well-dressed pedestrians

A SENSE OF BELONGING TO A MORAL ORDER AND BEING RIGHT IN WHAT ONE DOES, BEING IN AND OF A SYSTEM OF VALUES

Neighborhood stores in poor condition

Lack of morale and mutual responsibility

Uncontrollable minors

Danger of street assault

No historic character; no opportunity to express desire for continuity of local tradition and life style

Dirty and poorly maintained dwellings

Instability, changing use

High rate of turnover of residents; impermanency, transiency
Threat of eminent domain

List 2.   Elements needed on a residential site

PHYSICAL SECURITY
Ready access to utility and mechanical services
Sheltered access from house to parked car
Visual observation of children playing outside by mother
Means of limiting outside area where children are playing
Means of securing possible entry points into unoccupied units
from penetration by children, youth, and vandals
Reducing speed of vehicles entering housing areas
Control of vehicles for the safety of children
Separation of children's playing areas from places of heavy
vehicular traffic
Emergency vehicle access to dwelling units

SEXUAL SATISFACTION
Acoustical insulation of sleeping spaces

THE EXPRESSION OF HOSTILITY
None

THE EXPRESSION OF LOVE
Visual observation of children playing outside by mother

THE SECURING OF LOVE
None

THE EXPRESSION OF SPONTANEITY
Parking space available for other uses
Provision for retiring early even if others are still around
Some private outdoor areas for each family unit
Quiet place for children to read, study, or talk uninterrupted

THE SECURING OF RECOGNITION
None

ORIENTATION IN TERMS OF ONE'S PLACE IN SOCIETY AND THE PLACES
OF OTHERS
Provision for waste collection out of public view
Clear definition of the areas of occupancy that the occupant is
solely responsible for in terms of physical maintenance
Clear definition of semi-public domain (that part of private
domain which the public is allowed the use of either physically
or visually)
Observation of people at the entry by people within
Entry into dwelling without coming into contact with others

Easy recognition of all public facilities

Clear definition of public domains

THE SECURING AND MAINTAINING OF MEMBERSHIP IN A DEFINITE
HUMAN GROUP

Provision of a pubic place outside the realm of the dwelling
where people can meet when the weather is good

Place for people to sit passively and observe interaction of other
groups

Individual family to identify with a community unit

A SENSE OF BELONGING TO A MORAL ORDER AND BEING RIGHT IN WHAT
ONE DOES, BEING IN AND OF A SYSTEM OF VALUES

None

Selected Bibliography

The works listed here do not duplicate those cited in footnotes.

Bachelard, Gaston.
The Poetics of Space. Boston: Beacon Press, 1969.

Banham, Reyner.
The New Brutalism. London: The Architectural Press, 1966.

Banton, Michael, ed.
The Relevance of Models for Social Anthropology. London: Tavistock Publications, 1965.

———, ed.
The Social Anthropology of Complex Societies. London: Tavistock Publications, 1966.

Beazley, Elizabeth.
Design and Detail of the Space Between Buildings. London: The Architectural Press, 1960.

Berelson, Bernard, and Steiner, Gary A.
Human Behavior: An Inventory of Scientific Findings. New York: Harcourt Brace & World, 1964.

Beyer, Glenn H.
Housing and Personal Values. Cornell University, Agricultural Experiment Station, Memoir 364, 1959.

———, ed.
The Cornell Kitchen. Cornell University, 1952.

Bloom, Martin.
"Life Span Analysis: A Theoretical Framework for Behavioral Science Research." *Journal of Human Relations,* Vol. 12, No. 4, 1964, pp. 538–554.

Boyd, Robin.
The Puzzle of Architecture. London: Cambridge University Press, 1965.

Brown, Robert.
Explanation in Social Science. Chicago: Aldine Publishing Co., 1963.

Building Research Institute.
"Effect of Buildings on Human Behavior." *Building Research,* July-August 1965, pp. 3–18.

Carroll, Michael A.
"An Exploration of the Relationship Between Urban Planning and Human Behavior: Toward the Identification of Professional Responsibilities." Exchange Bibliography 60, Council of Planning Librarians, October 1968.

Cook, Peter.
Architecture: Action and Plan. New York: Reinhold Publishing Corp., 1967.

Cox, Oliver.
"Professional Obsolescence." *Arena,* June 1966, unpaged.

————.
"Brief Making in Action." *Northern Architect,* December 1966, unpaged.

Dahir, James.
The Neighborhood Unit Plan: Its Spread and Acceptance. New York: Russell Sage Foundation, 1947.

Dober, Richard P.
Environmental Design. New York: Van Nostrand Reinhold, 1969.

Dreyfuss, Henry.
The Measure of Man: Human Factors in Design. Second edition. New York: Whitney Library of Design, 1968.

Dubos, René.
Man Adapting. New Haven and London: Yale University Press, 1965.

Erikson, Erik H.
Childhood and Society. New York: Norton, 1950.

Fuller, R. Buckminster.
Operating Manual for Spaceship Earth. Carbondale: Southern Illinois University Press, 1969.

Gans, Herbert J.
"Social and Physical Planning for the Elimination of Urban Poverty," in *Urban Planning and Social Policy,* ed. Bernard J. Frieden and Robert Morris. New York: Basic Books, 1968.

Gibberd, Frederick.
Town Design. London: The Architectural Press, 1962.

Glaser, Barney G., and Strauss, Anselm L.
The Discovery of Grounded Theory: Strategies for Qualitative Research. London: Weidenfeld and Nicolson, 1968.

Goffman, Erving.
Behavior in Public Places: Notes on the Social Organization of Gatherings. New York: Free Press, 1963.

————.
Interaction Ritual: Essays in Face-To-Face Behavior. Chicago: Aldine Publishing Company, 1967.

Goodman, Paul.
Utopian Essays and Practical Proposals. New York: Vintage Books, 1962.

————.
People or Personnel and *Like a Conquered Province.* New York: Vintage Books, 1968.

Gropius, Walter.
Scope of Total Architecture. New York: Collier Books, 1962.

_____. *The New Architecture and the Bauhaus.* Cambridge, Mass.: The M.I.T. Press, 1965.

Gutman, Robert.
"A Sociologist Looks at Housing." ed. Daniel P. Moynihan, *Toward a National Urban Policy.* New York: Basic Books, 1969.

_____. "The Social Function of the Built Environment." Paper #8, Urban Studies Center, Rutgers University, mimeo. January 8, 1968.

_____. "Notes on the Professionalization of Architecture." *Connection,* Vol. 5, Nos. 2 and 3, Winter-Spring, 1968, pp. 76–78.

_____. "Library Architecture and People." ed. Ernest de Prospo, Jr. *The Library Building Consultant.* New Brunswick, N.J.: Rutgers University Press, 1969, pp. 11–29.

_____. "Urban Transporters as Human Environments." *Journal of the Franklin Institute,* Vol. 286, No. 5, November 1968, pp. 533–539.

_____. "Sociology in Architectural Education." 1966 AIA Architect-Researcher's Conference. Washington, D.C.: American Institute of Architects, 1966, pp. 5–17.

_____. "The Social Effects of the Urban Environment." Center for Urban Social Science Research, Rutgers University, October 1969.

Guttenberg, Albert Z.
The Social Evaluation of Non-Residential Land Use: Substandardness Criteria. Urbana: University of Illinois, Bureau of Community Planning, 1967.

Hall, Edward T.
The Hidden Dimension. New York: Doubleday & Co., 1966.

_____. *The Silent Language.* New York: Doubleday & Co., 1959.

Hammond, Phillip E., ed.
Sociologists at Work. New York: Anchor Books, 1967.

Higgin, Garth, and Jessop, Neil.
Communications in the Building Industry. London: Tavistock Publications, 1965.

Hughes, H. Stuart.
Consciousness and Society: The Reorientation of European Social Thought 1890–1930. New York: Alfred A. Knopf, 1961.

Kira, Alexander.
The Bathroom: Criteria for Design. Center for Housing and Environmental Studies, Cornell University, 1966.

Lemkau, Paul V.
Mental Hygiene in Public Health. New York: McGraw-Hill, 1949.

Lowenthal, David, ed.
Environmental Perception and Behavior. Chicago: University of Chicago, Department of Geography, Research Paper No. 109, 1967.

Lynd, Robert S.
Knowledge for What? The Place of Social Science in American Culture. Princeton: Princeton University Press, 1939.

Madge, John.
"Privacy and Social Interaction." *Transactions of the Bartlett Society, Volume 3,* pp. 123–141. London: Bartlett School of Architecture, University College, 1964–65.

Mannheim, Karl.
Systematic Sociology: An Introduction to the Study of Society. New York: Grove Press, 1957.

Manning, Peter.
"Appraisals of Building Performance: Their Use in the Design Process." *The Architects' Journal,* October 9, 1968, pp. 793–800.

Markus, Thomas A.
"The Role of Building Performance Measurement and Appraisal in Design Method," *The Architect's Journal,* 20 December 1967, pp. 1567–1573.

Marris, Peter, and Rein, Martin.
Dilemmas of Social Reform. New York: Atherton Press, 1967.

Masserman, Jules H.
The Biodynamic Roots of Human Behavior. Springfield: Charles C Thomas, 1968.

Mayer, Albert.
"Public Housing Architecture Evaluated from PWA Days up to 1962," *Journal of Housing,* Vol. 19, No. 8, October 15, 1962, pp. 446–468.

————.
"Public Housing Design," *Journal of Housing,* Vol. 20, No. 3, April 12, 1963, pp. 133–144.

Mackinnon, Donald W.
"The Study of Creative Persons: A Method and Some Results." ed. Jerome Kagan, *Creativity and Learning.* Boston: Houghton Mifflin, 1967.

McGrath, Joseph E., and Altman, Irwin.
Small Group Research. New York: Holt, Rinehart & Winston, 1966.

Mead, Margaret.
"The City as a Point of Confrontation" and "Megalopolis: Is it Inevitable?" *Transactions of the Bartlett Society, Volume 3,*

pp. 9–41. London: Bartlett School of Architecture, University College, 1964–65.

———, ed.
Cultural Patterns and Technical Change. Paris: UNESCO, 1953.

Meier, Richard L.
"The Metropolis as a Transaction-Maximizing System." *Daedalus,* Fall 1968, pp. 1292–1313.

Meyer, Leonard B.
Music, the Arts, and Ideas. Chicago: University of Chicago Press, 1967.

Michelson, William.
"The Physical Environment as Attraction and Determinant: Social Effects in Housing." Research Paper 22, Centre for Urban and Community Studies, University of Toronto, 1969.

———.
"Selected Aspects of Environmental Research in Scandinavia," draft, Department of Sociology, University of Toronto.

Miller, R. B.
"Task Taxonomy: Science or Technology?" in *Proceedings of the Conference on the Human Operator in Complex Systems,* eds., Singleton, Easterby, Whitfield. London: Taylor & Francis, 1967, pp. 67–76.

Mills, C. Wright.
The Sociological Imagination. New York: Grove Press, 1961.

Ministry of Housing and Local Government (Welsh Office).
The Needs of New Communities: A Report on Social Provision in New and Expanding Communities. London: Her Majesty's Stationery Office, 1967.

Moller, Clifford B.
Architectural Environment and Our Mental Health. New York: Horizon Press, 1968.

Murray, Henry A., and Kluckhohn, Clyde.
"Outline of a Conception of Personality" in *Personality in Nature, Society, and Culture,* ed. Clyde Kluckhohn, Henry A. Murray and David M. Schneider. Second edition. New York: Alfred A. Knopf, 1967.

Murrell, K. F. H.
Ergonomics: Man in His Working Environment. London: Chapman and Hall, 1965.

Myrick, Richard.
"New Concept in Architectural Planning for Schools of Dentistry." *Journal of Dental Education,* Vol. 29, No. 4, December 1965, pp. 382–386.

Nagel, Ernest.
The Structure of Science: Problems in the Logic of Scientific Explanation. New York: Harcourt, Brace & World, 1961.

Nelson, George.
Problems of Design. New York: Whitney Publications, 1965.

Peattie, Lisa R.
"Reflections on Advocacy Planning." *Journal of the American Institute of Planners,* Vol. 34, No. 2, March 1968, pp. 80–88.

————.
"The Social Anthropologist in Planning." *Journal of the American Institute of Planners,* Vol. 33, No. 4, July 1967, pp. 266–268.

Perin, Constance.
"Some Interests of the City Planner in Social Science Research." *Journal of the American Institute of Planners,* Vol. 33, No. 2, March 1967, pp. 114–116.

Perlman, Robert.
"Social Welfare Planning and Physical Planning." *Journal of the American Institute of Planners,* Vol. 32, No. 4, July 1966, pp. 237–241.

Rapoport, Rhona, and Rapoport, Robert.
"Family Transitions in Contemporary Society." *Journal of Psychosomatic Research,* Vol. 12, 1968, pp. 29–38.

Ratcliff, Richard U.
"Housing Standards and Housing Research." *Land Economics,* Vol. 28, No. 4, November 1952, pp. 328–332.

Ritter, Paul.
Educreation: Education for Creation, Growth and Change. Oxford: Pergamon Press, 1966.

Rosenberg, Gerhard.
"City Planning Theory and the Quality of Life." *The American Behavioral Scientist,* December 1965–January 1966, pp. 3–7.

Ruesch, Jurgen.
"Social Psychiatry: An Overview." *Archives of General Psychiatry,* Vol. 12 (5), May 1965, pp. 501–509.

Schermer, George Associates.
More Than Shelter: Social Needs in Low- and Moderate-Income Housing. Washington: GPO 1968 (Research Report No. 8, National Commission on Urban Problems).

Schneider, David M.
American Kinship: A Cultural Account. Englewood Cliffs, N.J.: Prentice-Hall, 1968.

Searles, Harold F.
The Nonhuman Environment in Normal Development and in Schizophrenia. New York: International Universities Press, 1960.

Skinner, B. F.
Science and Human Behavior. New York: Free Press Paperback, 1965.

Smith, M. Brewster.
Social Psychology and Human Values. Chicago: Aldine Publishing Company, 1969 (especially the chapter "Competence and Socialization," pp. 210–250).

Sorokin, Pitrim A., and Berger, Clarence Q.
Time-Budgets of Human Behavior. Cambridge, Mass.: Harvard University Press, 1939.

UNESCO
International Social Science Journal. "Multidisciplinary Problem-Focused Research." Vol. XX, No. 2, 1968.

U.S. Department of Housing and Urban Development.
Tomorrow's Transportation: New Systems for the Urban Future. Washington: GPO, 1968.

van Ettinger, J.
Decision Making and Functional Principles of Housing. Bouwcentrum, Rotterdam, January 1970.

Venturi, Robert.
Complexity and Contradiction in Architecture. New York: Museum of Modern Art, 1966.

Vidich, Arthur J., Bensman, Joseph, and Stein, Maurice R.
Reflections on Community Studies. New York: John Wiley and Sons, 1964.

von Mering, Otto.
A Grammar of Human Values. Pittsburgh, University of Pittsburgh Press, 1961.

Wax, Murray L.
"The Tree of Social Knowledge." *Psychiatry*, Vol. 28, No. 2, May 1965, pp. 99–106.

Webb, Eugene J., Campbell, Donald T., Schwartz, Richard D., and Sechrest, Lee.
Unobtrusive Measures: Nonreactive Research in the Social Sciences. Chicago: Rand McNally & Co., 1966.

Wells, Brian W. P.
"The Psycho-Social Influence of Building Environment: Sociometric Findings in Large and Small Office Spaces." *Building Science*, Vol. 1, 1965, pp. 153–165 (Great Britain).

———.
"Subjective Responses to the Lighting Installation in a Modern Office Building and Their Design Implications." *Building Science*, Vol. 1, 1965, pp. 57–68.

White, Robert W.
"Motivation Reconsidered: The Concept of Competence," in Fiske and Maddi, *Functions of Varied Experience*. Homewood, Ill.: The Dorsey Press, 1961, pp. 278–325.

White, Richard W.
"A Study of the Relationship Between Mental Health and Residential Environment," Thesis submitted for the Master's in City Planning Degree, Department of City and Regional Planning, Massachusetts Institute of Technology, awarded September 1957.

Whiting, John W. M., Child, Irvin L., and Lambert, William W.
Field Guide for a Study of Socialization. New York: John Wiley and Sons, 1966.

Wiener, Norbert.
The Human Use of Human Beings. Second edition. New York: Doubleday Anchor, 1954.

Willmott, Peter.
"Social Research and New Communities." *Journal of the American Institute of Planners,* Vol. 33, No. 6, November 1967, pp. 387–398.

Wood, Elizabeth.
"Social Goals for Low, Moderate-Income Housing Management Defined." *The Journal of Housing,* No. 5, 1967, unpaged.

Wright, Frank Lloyd.
The Natural House. New York: Horizon House, 1954.

Zajonc, Robert B. and Sales, Stephen M.
"Social Facilitation of Dominant and Subordinate Responses." *Journal of American Social Psychology,* Vol. 2, No. 2, April 1966, pp. 160–168.

Znaniecki, Florian.
Cultural Sciences: Their Origin and Development. Urbana: University of Illinois Press, 1952.

Index